KYKUIT

THE HOUSE AND GARDENS

of the ROCKEFELLER FAMILY

HENRY JOYCE

SECOND EDITION
ADDITIONAL TEXT
Cynthia Bronson Altman
Susan T. Greenstein

HISTORIC HUDSON VALLEY

KYKUIT IS A PROPERTY OF THE NATIONAL TRUST FOR HISTORIC PRESERVATION
AND IS OPERATED AND MAINTAINED BY THE ROCKEFELLER BROTHERS FUND AS A CENTER
FOR ITS PHILANTHROPIC PROGRAMS. HISTORIC HUDSON VALLEY, A NETWORK OF SIX
HISTORIC SITES, ADMINISTERS PUBLIC PROGRAMS AT KYKUIT.

CONTENTS

© HISTORIC HUDSON VALLEY PRESS, 1994; UPDATED AND REPRINTED, 2005   ISBN 0-912882-95-6
Design: Steven Schoenfelder   Printed in Italy by Conti Tipocolor
Illustrations on the inside front and inside back cover are from a folio of limited edition prints,
12 Historic Homes in the Hudson Valley, courtesy of the artist, George Ellsworth Shear, www.ARCHistration.com

FOREWORD

It is my pleasure to welcome you to Kykuit, home to four generations of the Rockefeller family. Kykuit and Pocantico Hills are very special to me; I lived at Kykuit with my Mom and Dad and brother, Nelson, on weekends, many holidays and during much of the summer months in my formative years, until I was twelve. When we were young boys, my brother and I went to school in New York City, and on Friday afternoons we would get in the car and travel up to Pocantico Hills. These times, which I remember so fondly, were about family, and our friends, and the joys of living in Pocantico and Westchester County.

During the day, my brother and I often played in the inner garden. My parents put in a swimming pool for adults and a shallow pool that was half pool and half sandbox for all the children in our extended family. (Both pools have since been removed, returning those central spaces to a sunken lawn, as they were in Grandfather's day.)

We enjoyed riding our big wheels and skateboards all around the terraces. I also recall swinging in one of the two hammocks strung between the Linden trees. Lunch was often served on the south-facing terrace overlooking the swimming pools, and we sat in the chairs that are similar to the ones now on the terrace. Mom and Dad installed an ice cream soda fountain in the teahouse that overlooks the inner garden, which was great fun. They both believed that Kykuit was a place to enjoy without any pretensions, and so a soda fountain in my great grandmother's tea house did not seem out of place.

My brother Nelson and I sometimes invited friends for the weekend, and we'd play football and baseball in the oval in front of the house. A ball hit over the high stone wall into the morning garden was a home run. Although I don't recall breaking any windows, there was always that possibility.

We often had family dinners, just the four of us, at the round iron table on the terrace overlooking the Hudson River. Every so often, summer thunderstorms rolled up the river in the early evening. I'll always remember watching those dramatic scenes, with the fast-moving, black clouds and streaks of lightening darting across the stormy sky. I remember feeling excited by the storms, but perfectly safe with my family and the protection of the covered patios. Another wonderful memory is of several July 4th celebrations with the family at Kykuit, where we'd go up on the roof to watch the fireworks displays up and down the Hudson. This great view of such patriotic and exciting festivities created, for me, a real sense of the sweep and majesty of the river and the Hudson Valley.

As a young child, I loved and appreciated Kykuit as my home; I never thought of it as a historic site to be preserved and protected. Dad put some of the more breakable pieces of art in Plexiglas cases, but that was to allow us to run and play in the house and to free him from worry about our breaking these beautiful pieces of art. My parents lived with the art in a casual and relaxed way, so we grew up appreciating it's beauty. That in itself was a great privilege.

The room now called the office was essentially our family room. Dad installed a television behind a false wall of leather-bound books and watched the news, and as children we would watch sports or favorite shows while Dad did paperwork or read reports. Across the hall in the drawing room, there was—and still is—a round table where my brother Nelson and I played pick-up-sticks with Mom and Dad.

Another very fond memory is spending most Christmases at Kykuit. One year there was a huge tree in the music room, rising to the second floor, but most years the tree was in front of the big picture window where the Bodhisattva stands. We hung our stockings in the music room and fires crackled in the fireplaces.

My parents entertained at Kykuit, more than was done by my grandfather and certainly more than by my great-grandfather. Being a young child, my memories of my parents' social events are hazy, but I'm aware that many important political figures visited, including Emperor Hiro Hito of Japan, King Hussein of Jordan, Egypt's Anwar Sadat, Ronald and Nancy Reagan, before he became President, as well as Presidents Johnson, Nixon, and Ford. I remember helicopters coming and going from the lawn in front of the Adam and Eve fountain, below the forecourt. Sometimes, my brother Nelson and I went to New York by helicopter with Dad. One time after Dad landed at the Adam and Eve sculpture area, the helicopter took off again, and we flew to a nearby lake, landed there, and then flew back. That was certainly great fun!

Although these are exciting memories, equally if not more memorable to a young boy was the time we spent in the outdoors, camping, fishing, and especially antique bottle-hunting on some of our family property. Dad would show us places where we could excavate, and off we'd go. We uncovered some amazing old bottles in our archeological pursuits, and then we'd go down to the sub-basement, where there was a big sink. We'd clean the bottles and look up the designs in books. It was a great treasure hunt. One day, Dad picked out a selection of our found bottles, and working together we arranged them in a glass case that is still displayed in the gallery downstairs. I think Dad was trying to teach us about art and history in a way that we children could understand and find relevant. These simple childhood experiences may have influenced me to major in history when I went to Princeton. I plan to start bottle excavating with my children, as soon as they're old enough, and I hope that they will enjoy the experience as much as I did.

I was probably influenced more by the landscape and open space surrounding Kykuit than I was by the house itself. I now have a deep and abiding love for the outdoors and conservation, which I believe stems from my outdoor weekend adventures, including bottle hunting.

As a young child, I enjoyed our overnight camping trips into the woods at Pocantico. Mom, Dad, Nelson, and I would often camp out in the woods. We'd fish for largemouth bass and sunnies and then cook our supper outdoors too.

Now as an adult, when I look across the landscape from Kykuit to the Palisades, and when I walk in the part of my grandfather's estate that is now the Rockefeller State Park Preserve, I think about the value and public benefit of preserving natural landscapes. I respect in particular the vision of my grandfather, John D. Rockefeller, Jr., who lived at Kykuit before we did, and of my Uncle Laurance, who died recently, as well as the commitment of so many family members, now and in the previous generations, to preservation of open space. Their legacy of conservation and philanthropic enterprise, here in the Hudson Valley and all across the United States, comes alive for me throughout Pocantico Hills—at Kykuit, at the new Stone Barns Center, and at the Park Preserve—as I hope it does for many visitors.

I'm happy that the family made the decision that we did to preserve Kykuit as a historic site, where visitors could share in the beauty of the landscape and enjoy the architecture, gardens, art, and history represented at Kykuit. I have never thought of it as a monument to my family. I know that has never been the goal.

I believe it was inevitable that Kykuit would become something to share, welcoming visitors from all over the world. I know that my father intended this; he even expressed his wish that it would be operated by Historic Hudson Valley, the organization founded by his father, JDR, Jr., as Sleepy Hollow Restorations. Indeed, Dad's goal was that Kykuit be interpreted as a historic site "reflecting the lives of three generations of the Rockefeller family and their interests."

Today, the Rockefeller Brothers Fund maintains Kykuit and operates a small conference center in the lower level of the Coach Barn, through an arrangement with the National Trust for Historic Preservation, which owns the site. The RBF's focus is on continuing the family's philanthropic endeavors and convening people who concentrate on major national and international issues. The interpretation of Kykuit—its history, art, architecture, landscape, and the family's legacy—is the responsibility of Historic Hudson Valley. It was certainly the hope of Dad's generation that the important work of the family be perpetuated through the partnership of these three non-profit organizations, collaborating together in the spirit of the public good. I'm delighted to have a part in fulfilling their vision and pleased to share all of this with you. I hope you enjoy your visit and return as often as you like to share the myriad delights that Kykuit has to offer.

Mark F. Rockefeller
Chairman, Historic Hudson Valley
May, 2005

INTRODUCTION

For a hundred years—and now for six generations—our family has lived here on this part of the Hudson.
We are very pleased that others will be able to visit this historic site and share the wonders of its surroundings.

— DAVID ROCKEFELLER

Since its construction between 1906 and 1913, Kykuit has been the principal home of the family and descendants of John D. Rockefeller. Rockefeller (often referred to in this guidebook as JDR) was the founder of the Standard Oil Company, one of the largest industrial enterprises of its time. A forerunner of the modern American corporation, Standard Oil and other companies such as U.S. Steel and the American Telephone and Telegraph Company built the United States into a global leader in industrial production around the turn of the twentieth century.

John D. Rockefeller was, in addition, perhaps the most significant philanthropist the United States has ever produced. His philanthropy distinguished him from most other great industrialists; in this century, JDR gave to charitable and other causes to a degree never before seen and rarely if ever matched. His son, John D. Rockefeller, Jr. (here referred to as Junior), continued his philanthropic work, as do his surviving grandchildren and great-grandchildren.

John D. Rockefeller used Kykuit to escape from the rigors of New York City life until his death in 1937, when the home became a spring and fall retreat for his son and his son's wife, Abby Aldrich Rockefeller. After Junior's death in 1960, his second son, Nelson, then governor of New York State and later vice-president of the United States, lived at Kykuit until his death in 1979. He, his wife Margaretta ("Happy"), and their two sons Nelson, Jr. and Mark were the last Rockefellers to live in the house. Kykuit and the surrounding estate have provided a sense of continuity for six generations of Rockefellers. According to Nelson Rockefeller, Jr., family gatherings at this house over many decades "have been a source of unity, strength, and energy, qualities that made possible many significant accomplishments and contributions." People from all walks of life, including artists, teachers, and religious and political leaders, have been guests at Kykuit; members of the family have exchanged ideas here with experts and leaders in many different fields from around the world.

In 1976, Kykuit was declared a National Historic Landmark. Three years later, Nelson Rockefeller's will left his share of what had been his grandfather's estate to the National Trust for Historic Preservation. By agreement with the National Trust, the Rockefeller Brothers Fund manages the Pocantico Historic Area, which includes Kykuit, its gardens, and the coach barn. Kykuit serves as a center for the Fund's philanthropic programs. Historic Hudson Valley, founded by John D. Rockefeller, Jr. in 1951 as Sleepy Hollow Restorations, operates the property's visitor services and interpretation programs.

John D. Rockefeller at Kykuit with (left to right) John D. Rockefeller, Jr., Abby Aldrich Rockefeller, Laurance S. Rockefeller, Winthrop Rockefeller (in front of pillar), Abby (Babs) Rockefeller, and Nelson A. Rockefeller, about 1935.

THE ROCKEFELLERS AND KYKUIT

*B*orn on a farm in upstate New York in 1839 and raised in Cleveland, John D. Rockefeller had built Standard Oil into one of the country's most successful corporations before he was forty years old. While living in Cleveland, he had purchased a nearby rural retreat called Forest Hill, which he used in the summer months. But within a decade of his move to New York City in 1884, he began to seek a place in the countryside where he and his family could spend the spring and fall. In 1893, JDR purchased four hundred acres at Pocantico Hills, a parcel that would ultimately grow to more than two thousand acres by the turn of the century.

JDR's initial purchase included Kykuit Hill, an exposed hilltop site five hundred feet above sea level. Dutch colonists had named the hill Kykuit (pronounced pie-cut), which means "lookout," for its panoramic view of the Hudson River. Although JDR and his family continued to spend summers at Forest Hill until the First World War, they often stayed at Kykuit in the Parsons-Wentworth house, which stood near the present-day coach barn, until it burned in 1902. After the fire, JDR moved to another residence on the property, but its limited river view inspired his son, then in his late twenties, to urge JDR to build a new house that would take advantage of the property's spectacular views of the river and the Palisades. Junior also believed his father should have designed for himself a house appropriate to his stature as one of the country's leading industrialists and philanthropists.

JDR had at different times entertained the notion of building on the hilltop site, but he seemed in no hurry to act even after the Parsons-Wentworth house burned. He had often bought properties on which dwellings already existed, including his New York City townhouse and his Forest Hill country house outside Cleveland. Thus, Rockefeller may not have been greatly interested in the idea of new construction. Furthermore, in 1901, he had purchased a golf course and former clubhouse in Lakewood, New Jersey. Absorbed as he was with alterations at Lakewood, JDR made no immediate plans to build a house at Kykuit.

John D. Rockefeller, Jr. Moves Forward on the Project

JDR, Jr. remained committed to the idea. In 1902, without his father's knowledge, Junior asked the architect Chester Holmes Aldrich (1871–1940), a friend and distant cousin of his wife Abby, to draw up plans. Aldrich and his partner, William Adams Delano (1874–1960), had both earlier worked at Carrère and Hastings, the architectural firm that had transformed the home of JDR's brother William into the largest and most glamorous Hudson River mansion of the 1880s. William Rockefeller, Standard Oil's agent for overseas exports, had named the home Rockwood Hall. Located just north of Tarrytown, it was razed in the 1940s.

Meanwhile, JDR began at last to talk to architects about building a house on his Tarrytown property. He asked Dunham A. Wheeler (1867-1938), the architect he had hired for the Lakewood clubhouse and the son of well-known designer Candace Wheeler, to prepare preliminary sketches for Kykuit. Delano and Aldrich ultimately became Kykuit's first architects, but because JDR wanted a relatively unassuming house designed for comfort and not for show he insisted that Wheeler's modest T-shaped ground-floor plan be used as the basis for the new residence. This requirement certainly accounts for Kykuit's close arrangement of moderately sized rooms; Delano and Aldrich's other country houses routinely featured a more generous scale. Junior's idea to make a significant and dignified impression appropriate to the Rockefeller name was thus restrained considerably by JDR's mandate.

Junior Takes the Lead

By the spring of 1904, JDR permitted his son to take the lead in preparing the plans, and two years later, as the cellars for Kykuit were being excavated, Junior took full command of the job. He acted as client, general contractor, and clerk of the works, writing and calling architects, contractors, and supply companies on a daily basis, overseeing virtually every detail, large and small, of design and construction. He even wrote to the president of U.S. Steel to request that deliveries to the site be expedited. Kykuit

The house and west terrace nearing completion (first phase), January 1908.

was one of the first major responsibilities that Junior had taken on for his father, and although they sometimes disagreed about how Kykuit should look the project probably played a large role in how he earned his father's trust. Afterward, he began to assume a greater share of the family's business and philanthropic concerns.

While his father and mother were in Europe, Junior hired William Welles Bosworth (1869–1966) to design the extensive gardens, and Ogden Codman, Jr. (1862–1951), one of the foremost exponents of the classical revival in America, to design the interiors. Ultimately both determined more of Kykuit's final appearance than Delano and Aldrich, who quickly became involved with new commissions that earned their reputation as New York's leading country house architects.

In 1906, Bosworth's work was neither extensive nor well-known. His gardens at Kykuit, which survive virtually unchanged, are generally considered his best. Junior came to trust Bosworth's artistic judgment and continued to seek his ideas for the grounds at Kykuit through the early 1920s. By the time they were finished, the gardens had become more elaborate and complex than the house.

Indeed, father and son shared an interest in gardening and the landscape; they differed about, and were ultimately less interested in, the house.

Unlike Bosworth, Codman was already well-established when Junior hired him. His work in and around Boston, Newport, and New York was widely known and much admired. Junior knew the architect's own house in New York City and made a New England tour specifically to see his interiors. Codman's 1897 book *The Decoration of Houses,* co-written with the novelist Edith Wharton, greatly influenced the move away from the overstuffed and overdraped Victorian interiors of a generation earlier toward the clean, rational, and relatively uncluttered lines of the classical revival style. The interiors of many fine turn-of-the-century American houses reflected this transition, not least of all Kykuit: one 1909 article in *House Beautiful* declared that Kykuit's drawing room was "entirely removed from the elaborate and overdone schemes often found in the homes of American millionaires."

The classical revival emulated the design principles of the ancient cultures of Greece and Rome and of Renaissance Italy, widely viewed as the greatest intellectual and cultural

Kykuit entrance façade by Delano and Aldrich, completed in 1908, subsequently redesigned by William Welles Bosworth and Ogden Codman, Jr.

traditions of the western world. Designing Kykuit in this style, Junior clearly believed, instantly associated his family with these ideas. Though Delano and Aldrich thought that he had compromised their position as principal architects by hiring Codman, Junior ultimately managed to negotiate the collaboration of all of the designers through two distinct design and building phases, the first from 1906 to 1908 and the second from 1911 to 1913. Landscape designer Bosworth, for example, actually redesigned the Kykuit façade after extensive consultation with Codman, whose influence was pivotal in both phases. The rooms Codman designed for Kykuit are fine examples of his style and demonstrate his interest in creating an essential unity in all the details of a room. Junior depended upon him for many decisions about his father's furniture, curtains, carpets, and such decorative objects as silver and ceramics. Codman personally selected and purchased many of the furnishings in London and Paris. He also approved for use at Kykuit many of the furnishings that Junior and his wife Abby had acquired from various antique dealers in New York and Boston. Codman made sketches of room arrangements as well. The general style of these interiors changed very little during the

years that first JDR, later Junior, and finally Nelson and his family lived here.

Between 1906 and 1908, the Thompson-Starrett Company, better known for its skyscrapers in many American cities, undertook the first construction phase of Kykuit. Framed in steel, the house was designed in an eclectic style with a steep slate roof in the French manner but with colonial-revival-style porches opening onto Bosworth's formal gardens. Junior chose the decorating firm William Baumgarten and Company of New York City to implement Codman's interior designs; the company executed all interior plasterwork during both building phases and also supplied furnishings.

In poor health at the time, JDR's wife, Laura Spelman Rockefeller, was deliberately spared from the concerns of the building program; what Kykuit became was a matter negotiated principally by her husband and her only son. After Wheeler's plan was accepted, father and son communicated constantly, often by letter. As Kykuit neared completion in the summer of 1908, Junior and Abby lived in the house for about six weeks to put the finishing touches to the rooms—to give them, as Junior put it, the "lived in look." The summer

Classical-style pediment gracing the top of Kykuit's façade, with carvings by F. M. L. Tonetti, set underneath an American eagle cradling John D. Rockefeller's monogram.

also gave JDR's staff a chance to get to know the place. Junior asked his parents to stay at Forest Hill until the carpets arrived from Paris for the Kykuit living rooms. They finally arrived in October, within days of his parents' arrival.

But the experience of living at Kykuit that fall left the elder Mr. and Mrs. Rockefeller with serious reservations about the house. The third-floor guest bedrooms seemed too small, and the couple were dismayed by the smoking fireplaces and the noise from the kitchen delivery area, unfortunately placed on the north side of the house under JDR's bedroom window. Within little more than a year, they decided to make major changes.

Second Construction Phase Brings Major Changes

This second construction phase involved father and son in an extensive redesign. JDR and his wife moved out, and over the course of two years the walls of the third and fourth floors were raised, the façade was completely redesigned, and the entrance forecourt was lengthened to heighten its bold effect. Codman and Bosworth jointly came up with the idea for the new front, and JDR, who generally did not approve of Bosworth's extravagant tendencies, seems to have acquiesced in the plan. Bosworth's imposing classical façade complements both his pre-existing Italianate gardens and

Codman's classical interiors. Inside, Kykuit intentionally resembles a fine eighteenth-century English country house; it shows Codman's active borrowing from Christopher Wren for elements of the music room, from William Kent for the dining room and library, and from Robert Adam for the drawing room. At Kykuit, Codman wished to create the impression of an old family home filled with furniture acquired over generations. The house and garden thus were meant to evoke a sense of history by incorporating direct references to European precedents.

A detail of one of the many artful, decorative features designed by William Welles Bosworth.

Kykuit today bears evidence of both periods of its creation. The ground-floor rooms are little changed from 1908, but the exterior of the house, the raised garden covering a new tunnel to the service court (designed to muffle the noise of deliveries), and the large Oceanus fountain in the entrance forecourt date from the 1911–1913 redesign. After eight years, Junior believed he had at last created a house worthy of his father. In October 1913, when his parents moved back into Kykuit, they were both seventy-four years old. Laura Spelman Rockefeller died only two years later, but JDR enjoyed his new house even though it was grander than he had envisioned it. After 1917, when Forest Hill burned, Kykuit became his favorite home.

Third Generation at Kykuit

During Nelson and Happy Rockefeller's residency, Kykuit for the first time became a home with young children. Nelson Jr. and Mark grew up at Kykuit in a loving and supportive environment. Like many young boys, they enjoyed playing baseball and football, sometimes with their father in the east forecourt. In part of the south garden Nelson and Happy created a less formal family area with a bocce ball court, a swing, and other playground equipment. An avid gardener, Happy enjoyed teaching and sharing the pleasures of gardening, and the family often worked together in the vegetable garden. No rooms of the house, including the art galleries, were off-limits to these enthusiastic children, who learned early to appreciate and enjoy the art displayed throughout the house and gardens. The family lived with the art rather than regarding it with formal reverence.

Nelson Rockefeller loved people and was especially drawn to those who offered different perspectives on contemporary issues or creative approaches to solving problems. He and Happy frequently hosted dinners and receptions at Kykuit; notable people from worlds of politics, science, sports, and the arts often were guests. Nelson also met at Kykuit with his associates and his gubernatorial staff. The values of JDR's and Junior's time—a strong sense of family, evening prayers, stewardship, and an appreciation of beauty and aversion to ostentation—remained part of everyday life. JDR's and Junior's emphasis on building an unpretentious house on a human scale was still appreciated in Nelson's time.

In 1976, when Kykuit became a National Historic Landmark, Nelson Rockefeller said to President Ford at the dedication ceremony, "We, as a family, are deeply touched and moved that you are here on this occasion, because we are a very close family. My grandfather would be deeply moved if he knew the President of the United States was here. He grew up on a farm in upstate New York and worked his way from the time he was sixteen to help support his family and then do what he considered was the Lord's work."

The Italian Garden on the landing of the grand stairway. At the south end is Frederick Roth's 1919 replica of the ancient *Sleeping Ariadne* from the Vatican Collection along with cast stone figures representing the four seasons added by Nelson Rockefeller.

THE HOUSE

K ykuit is traditional in style but modern in technology. A generator in the coach barn brought electricity to the house, which was also equipped with central heating, a central vacuum system, an internal and external telephone system, and an Otis elevator. The elevator cab had an early push-button mechanism and a seat for Mrs. Rockefeller.

THE VESTIBULE

The pilasters around the stone walls of this entryway carry the classical theme from the exterior to the interior. Codman chose finely cut stonework, similar to that used on the carved details of the exterior to give emphasis to the area as a transitional space. Nelson Rockefeller added the three Chinese ceramic tomb figures of a horse, a groom, and a guardian; they date from T'ang Dynasty (618-906 A.D.). Nelson acquired them in the early 1970s; they attest to his passion for sculpture.

ABOVE: Chinese glazed tomb figures of a horse and attendant, T'ang Dynasty, early 8th Century, 22 inches high. These pieces were collected by Nelson Rockefeller and placed in plexiglas cases to protect them from any accidental damage by his two young sons and their friends in the busy front hall.

OPPOSITE: Entrance hall, designed by Ogden Codman, Jr. in 1907, completed in 1908, remains virtually unchanged today.

THE HALL

Somewhat more decorative than the vestibule, as the urns and putti above each door suggest, the hall introduces the English classical theme used throughout the house. The hall table is in the style of the furnishings designed by eighteenth-century English architect William Kent. Codman and Junior bought both antique and reproduction furniture in this style—much of it from Boston's A.H. Davenport Company, at the time the largest producer of fine furniture in the country—for all of Kykuit's rooms. Junior and his wife bought other furnishings from Koopman and Company in Boston, Tiffany Studios in New York, and English dealers with branches in the city, including Frank Partridge and Joseph Duveen.

The office looking east, with portrait of Benjamin Franklin over the fireplace. BELOW: Detail of the desk where John D. Rockefeller worked on his numerous philanthropic projects. Displayed on the desk today are many family photographs.

THE OFFICE

Offices used for business were not usually found in American country houses, but John D. Rockefeller's work ethic was so strong that it would have been inconceivable for him, even in retirement, not to have included such a space at Kykuit. He also needed a "working office" as a center for his growing philanthropic endeavors. It was here at Kykuit that his sense of charitable obligation fueled a growing commitment to "scientific giving," a commitment that led to JDR's status as one of the world's most effective philanthropists.

The small scale of the office reflects JDR's interest in making Kykuit a comparatively modest dwelling, but the classical pilasters around the walls display the architectural classicism Junior and Codman established for Kykuit generally. Before the room was finished in the fall of 1908, Junior wrote Codman that he wanted the color of the walls to be the same as that of a paneled room in Codman's own house in New York City. Originally the office upholstery

was a deep glowing red, as was the carpet; it was to appear traditional, dignified, and appropriate for a great businessman and philanthropist. The office has been its current color since the 1960s.

By 1908, when JDR began to use the room, he was sixty-nine years old. Yet when he was at Kykuit, he regularly worked in the office—usually after breakfast and before playing golf—until he died. The office had two desks, one at which JDR worked and another for his son or an associate. At this time in his life, the establishment of his philanthropic programs was one of his principal concerns, but JDR also met here with business visitors, including managers of the growing estate. During Nelson and Happy's years at Kykuit, the office was the family room. Here they and their children gathered before meals to catch up on the day's events, to read, or to watch television, especially football. Governor Rockefeller frequently read reports and correspondence in the large white chair by the fire.

THE DRAWING ROOM

In England and France in the eighteenth century, fine houses usually included drawing rooms specifically designed to reflect women's increasingly important role in society. In the United States in the nineteenth century, women making formal visits were welcomed in similar reception rooms, typically placed near the front entrance. After 1900 such rooms were considered old-fashioned, yet the elder Rockefellers, in their late sixties when Kykuit was built, may well have been attached to earlier ways.

The female associations of the room are evident in its elegant Sheraton-style furniture and its predominately cream-and-blue color scheme, almost certainly borrowed from the style of the eighteenth-century English architect Robert Adam. Codman specifically intended these choices to hark back to eighteenth-century England. The several portrait prints on the walls—including Lady Elizabeth Comp-

The drawing room was a favorite room of Abby Aldrich Rockefeller. Nelson Rockefeller added the gaming table, which once belonged to his grandfather, Senator Nelson W. Aldrich; Governor Rockefeller often played pick-up-sticks with his children and bridge with his wife, Happy, and their friends at this table. The Isfahan rug, early seventeenth century, came from Junior and Abby's New York City home.

The goose and tricorn are among the early Chinese ceramic figures from the Han and T'ang dynasties that Nelson Rockefeller added to the drawing room.

the acquisition of art and donated prints, sculpture, and paintings, including works by Matisse, Seurat, Degas, and Van Gogh. The museum's sculpture garden and print room are named for Mrs. Rockefeller, whose portrait by Frederick Wright hangs above the drawing room's satinwood commode. Nelson added the impressive collection of Chinese ceramic tomb sculptures, of the Han and T'ang dynasties. He and his family played bridge here; with his young sons, he often played "pick-up sticks." Sometimes called the "phone room," the governor also received and placed phone calls here.

THE MUSIC ROOM

The music room, Codman's most ambitious design at Kykuit, was modeled partly on the staircase hall of the seventeenth-century Ashburnham House in London, in the style of Sir Christopher Wren. Codman originally installed large double doors at the entrance to this room to separate the working or official part of the house (the office and the drawing room) from the more private family rooms. The music room is the first of these private rooms. The doors, two of eight pairs all around the room, had glass or mirror panes to reflect light. All but two were removed many years ago; the surviving pair, to the left of the fireplace, were covered to provide space for an abstract relief, Composition No. 68 by the noted Romanian sculptor Zoltan Kemeny (1907–1965), which Governor Rockefeller purchased in the 1960s.

A staircase rises behind the south wall of the music room, and the oval opening in the ceiling, called an oculus, with its balustrade and small dome above, reveals the second-floor gallery leading to bedrooms. Not an original feature of Delano and Aldrich's interior plan, the oculus and the dome

ton and Diana Viscountess Crosbie, both after paintings by Sir Joshua Reynolds—also make this association.

Seriously ill in her last years, Laura Spelman Rockefeller may not have used the drawing room very often; it is principally associated with Abby Aldrich Rockefeller, Junior's wife. In Nelson Rockefeller's day, the drawing room was known as "mother's room." From 1937 until her death in 1948, Abby sometimes used the drawing room to meet people who came to Kykuit in connection with the wide range of charitable and philanthropic activities in which she herself was involved. She may also have had meetings here about her collection of folk and modern art. Mrs. Rockefeller was one of the preeminent collectors of American folk art in this century; her collection is now part of Colonial Williamsburg, the restoration of which was funded largely by her husband. She was also one of three women collectors who founded the Museum of Modern Art (MoMA) in New York City. She gave MoMA its first fund for

Three Ming dynasty ceramic figures in the music room, probably made for a domestic altar, were part of John D. Rockefeller, Jr.'s collection.

The music room in 1908 with its original Aeolian organ. Sunlight streams through the French doors to the south and is reflected in the mirrored panels of the adjacent doors.

above it was one of Codman's ideas, and a costly one: it involved removing steel beams on the second and third floors and created construction delays that were a constant anxiety for Junior in 1907 and 1908.

A pipe organ and its console with three keyboards, made by the Aeolian Company of New York, were originally located on the staircase wall. Both JDR and his son enjoyed organ music, both religious and secular. When the elder Rockefellers occupied Kykuit, the organ was usually played after Sunday evening family dinners, sometimes by

H. R. Shelley, the organist at New York's Fifth Avenue Baptist Church; Shelley had helped design the Kykuit organ. In 1908, within weeks of moving into the house, Junior invited Shelley to play for his father's first Thanksgiving dinner here.

JDR's only documented requirement about any of the rooms appears in a letter to Shelley; the organ, he wrote, was to be "as extensive and as comprehensive as we could hope to have in the given space." The instrument could reproduce a wide range of orchestral sounds; pipes on the third floor produced a sound like church bells ringing in a steeple

From the second floor balcony through the oculus into the music room. The portrait of Senator Nelson W. Aldrich is by Swedish portraitist, Anders Zorn. Bradley Walker Tomlin's Number 5, 1959, hangs beyond the balustrade.

The music room today. Codman designed the oculus after one from the 1660s at Ashburnham House in London, near Westminster Abbey. The large painting over the sofa is a copy of the original *Hirondelle Amour,* 1933–34, by Joan Miro. After loaning the original for an exhibition, Nelson Rockefeller donated it to the Museum of Modern Art. Through the open doorway is a view of a Chinese Bodhisattva, T'ang dynasty.

high above. It also had a self-playing mechanism; nine times out of ten that the instrument was played, Junior recalled, it played music rolls—among them Edvard Grieg's *Peer Gynt,* one of the first rolls ever bought for the organ. In the 1960s, by which time the organ was in disrepair, Nelson Rockefeller had it removed (its whereabouts today is unknown). The original 1908 Steinway grand piano is still in the music room today.

Kykuit, unlike many large country houses of the period, has no ballroom. Strict Baptists who allowed no dancing or drinking in the house, John D. and Laura Rockefeller entertained only on a modest scale. Even the staircase in this room reflects a desire to avoid ostentation. In many fine houses of the time, grand staircases opening onto huge halls were built to facilitate a grand entrance. The staircase at Kykuit, hidden behind the organ wall, effectively concealed from view anyone using it and thus thwarted the vain display of fashionable clothes. Similarly, there is little

decorative gilding at Kykuit; most of the walls are white.

Junior collected the majority of the Chinese ceramics in the music room, many of which have been displayed at Kykuit since the late 1930s. A portrait painted in 1911 by Swedish artist Anders Zorn of his father-in-law, Rhode Island Senator Nelson W. Aldrich, hangs on the east wall; the large oil painting on the south wall, where the organ console once stood, is a replica of *Hirondelle Amour* by the great Spanish Surrealist Joan Miró. Nelson Rockefeller gave the original piece to the Museum of Modern Art in 1976; this copy has hung in the room since then. Governor Rockefeller believed that the colors of the picture harmonized with the Ming porcelains and the Chinese carpet. He also thought the glimpse of the modern paintings seen through the oculus has an intriguing, unexpected mystery about it; like his grandfather and father, he was drawn to the idea of creating interesting perspectives at Kykuit. The family's Christmas tree was often placed in this room.

The china room, created by Nelson Rockefeller to store and display the collections of china services, which include Spode and Worcester from England and Chinese export ware made for the European and American markets. Shown above are pieces from the Stowe service, Worcester, England, which was manufactured about 1815 for the Duke of Buckingham. The Duke's coat of arms is painted on each piece with a Latin motto that translates as "Such Splendid Temples," a pun on the Duke's family name of Temple.

THE CHINA ROOM

The china room was created out of three spaces in the original house—a coat storage room, a corridor that led to the north porch, and a small room where cut flowers from gardens were prepared for the house. Nelson Rockefeller created the room to display parts of nine dinner and dessert services he used during his years as governor and vice-president. The dinner service brightly decorated in pink and gold was made about 1815 for the Duke of Buckingham, whose magnificent coat of arms is painted on each piece. The service was made at the Worcester factory in England and is one of the best of its kind; it came to Kykuit in 1970. There are three Worcester services in this room, two from the Spode manufactory in England, and four made in China in the eighteenth or nineteenth centuries for the European and American export markets.

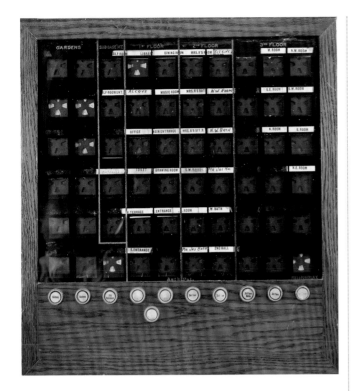

THE BUTLER'S PANTRY

Little-changed since it was finished in 1908, the butler's pantry is in many ways typical of pantries in other large houses of this era. Yet it is comparatively small, due to JDR's original requirement to build a modest house here.

Its scale makes it seem more like a pantry for a city townhouse than a spacious country estate.

During all three Rockefeller generations, the pantry was a center of operations for household staff. For Kykuit meals, food came up from the kitchen (on the ground floor directly below the pantry) in the dumbwaiter, which survives in this room along with the warming oven. The "annunciator station," original to the house, displayed the names of the rooms throughout the house. When an occupant of any room pushed its call button, an electrical signal rang a bell at the annunciator station and illuminated the name of the room. A houseman, household maid, or the lady's maid on duty would respond to the call from here or from the staff dining room on the ground floor, where another board was installed.

In JDR's time the household staff usually included a butler, a housekeeper, a valet, a cook, a cook's helper, two or three housemaids, and a first and second houseman. The housekeeper's room on the ground floor is now the curator's office. Servant's bedrooms on the fourth floor were separated into male and female sections, accessible by a common elevator with separate doors. The refrigerator in the pantry is from the 1970s, but there was refrigeration at Kykuit from the time the house was built. The ice plant was in the coach barn. The cupboards are for china and glass. In Governor Rockefeller's time the best ceramics were returned to their display cabinets in the china room.

ABOVE: Annunciator board in the butler's pantry with call buttons for various rooms in the house.

The kitchen (not on the tour), about 1908.

23

The dining room with its original Chippendale-style furniture. The portrait above the fireplace is of John D. Rockefeller, Jr., painted by Frank Salisbury in 1947. The portrait shown below is of John D. Rockefeller, painted by John Singer Sargent in 1917. It hangs above a table that displays two early Meissen bird figures, manufactured about 1730.

THE DINING ROOM

Codman based the design of the dining room and the adjoining alcove room and library on the general style of eighteenth-century English architect William Kent. The classical pediment of the overmantel and the marble fireplace mantel, with its architectural detailing and swags of grapes, are typical features of Kent's design. Codman used the decoration of the fireplace as the principal visual feature of the interior. He bought the marble mantel in England in 1907 from the well-known London firm of White, Allom and Company. The furniture, of the same date as the house, is also in English eighteenth-century style. The portrait of John D. Rockefeller above the Irish Chippendale-style console table was painted in 1917 by John Singer Sargent, one of America's foremost portraitists. The portrait of Junior above the fireplace was painted in 1947 by Frank Salisbury.

For JDR and later for Junior, Sunday dinner around this table with some of the children and grandchildren, was the most important family occasion of the week. Nelson and Happy continued these traditional family gatherings. Many world leaders have been entertained at Kykuit, including Prime Minister of Great Britain, Edward Heath; Presidents Lyndon Johnson and Richard Nixon; King Hussein of Jordan; and President Anwar Sadat of Egypt. When the house and estate were declared a National Historic Landmark in 1976, President Gerald Ford spoke at the dedication ceremony and dined here afterward. The last president to visit Kykuit was Ronald Reagan, who stayed here with his wife for two days in 1986 during the centennial celebration of the Statue of Liberty.

The alcove or tea room. The seventh-century Chinese Bodhisattva stands in front of the large double-hung window that opens to the west porch, which overlooks the Hudson River and Palisades. The portrait of Abby Aldrich Rockefeller, painted by Adele Herter in 1907, was a favorite of John D. Rockefeller, Jr.

THE ALCOVE ROOM

First used for afternoon tea, the alcove room was once called the tea room. The partial figure (from the T'ang dynasty) of a Bodhisattva, one of Buddha's divine attendants, once belonged to Abby Aldrich Rockefeller, whose portrait by Adele Herter hangs on the north wall. It was this Chinese marble figure, which once stood in the hall of the family's New York residence at 10 West 54th Street, that sparked what Nelson Rockefeller once termed his "artistic acquisitiveness," directed particularly toward sculpture. Nelson coupled the sculpture left to him in his mother's will with her portrait in the alcove room, perhaps to commemorate the origin of his lifelong avocation. In the pair of large display cabinets are Chinese ceramics of the Ming and Ching dynasties; these artifacts were a collecting passion for Junior, who began to assemble them when he purchased a large group from the estate of J.P. Morgan in 1915.

The library with its original furniture. The Chinese ceramic camel in front of the far window is from the T'ang dynasty; the portrait to its right is of George Washington by Gilbert Stuart. Over the fireplace is a portrait of Miss Judith Beresford by John Hoppner, circa 1785.

THE LIBRARY

In eighteenth-century England, William Kent was one of the first architects to design the libraries of fine English country houses to function as living rooms for the families of gentlemen educated in the classical arts and literature of Greece and Rome. Codman followed Kent's model at Kykuit.

John D. Rockefeller, Jr. was the first in his family to go to college. At Brown University in Providence, Rhode Island, he was steeped in the history, literature, and art of antiquity, the education thought appropriate for American gentlemen of his time. In this library Junior sought to create a serious-minded space that reflected the book-centered, classical values in which he had been trained. The classical pediment of the façade of the house is repeated here on the overmantel and bookcase. The small-scale pilasters in the overmantel decoration are reminiscent of eighteenth-century

high-style Rhode Island overmantels also based on Kent designs; Junior had almost certainly become aware of these overmantels in his student days, and his wife must have grown up among them in Providence.

The classical sensibility of the library is carried outdoors as well. The garden's north-south sight line runs through this room to center on a view of the south garden's Temple of Venus. Inside the temple is a replica of the famous Medici Venus at the Uffizi in Florence. When Junior bought the Venus, he was led to believe that it might be an original Greek sculpture by Praxiteles from the fourth century B. C. It is, in fact, an early nineteenth-century replica, but its association with the classical past is evident.

Portraits of George Washington by Gilbert Stuart and of Abraham Lincoln by Joseph Alexander Ames hang on the library walls, reinforcing the room's essentially cultural

Rodin's *Torso of Adele*, bronze, about 1882, sits on a corner table in the library.

Bookplate from the library of Abby and John D. Rockefeller, Jr. featuring an image of the Temple of Venus. The Temple of Venus can be seen through the south-facing library window.

function. But the comfortable furniture grouped around the fireplace indicates that the room was meant to be used by the whole family and that reading was a pastime as well as a serious pursuit. Nelson Rockefeller took another departure from the classical disposition of the room. The small bronze sculpture *Torso of Adele* of about 1882, purchased in the 1960s, is one of the earliest pieces in Nelson's collection and was viewed in its day as a radically anti-classical work. Sculpted by Auguste Rodin, considered the leader in the movement of sculpture away from its reliance on classical models, *Torso of Adele* shows the beginnings of sculpture's general tendency toward more abstract forms. It was also unusual in its time because it represented an active, female figure at a period when conventional sculpture associated action only with male figures.

A view of the inner garden, seen from the Moorish fountain, looking east toward the Italianate tea house. In the center of the canal is *Bather Putting up Her Hair* by Aristide Maillol, 1930, after a small figure of 1898.

THE INNER GARDEN & WEST PORCH

From the library, the southernmost room of the suite of private living rooms, French doors open directly on grade into the inner garden. Here the river view is shielded by a hundred-foot north-south allée of pleached linden trees, leading to double wrought-iron gates opening onto a path to the Temple of Venus.

Within the inner garden, the distinctive feature of the ensemble is the Italianate teahouse, with its pool and fountains in front. At the center of the linden tree allée is a Moorish-style basin lined with brass from the Gorham Company in Providence, perhaps better known for its silver tablewares. Its small, gilded bronze fountain, modeled by the sculptor F. M. L. Tonetti and cast by the Roman Bronze Company of New York, is of Orpheus in the midst of passion flowers. From here, a path of white marble leads eastward to the teahouse. A shallow canal twelve inches

The inner garden facing west to the Hudson River. In the center is the polished bronze, *Natura Extensa* by Peter Chinni, 1965; on the terrace wall to the right is George Kolbe's *Call of the Earth*, 1932.

BELOW: The inner garden in the early 1900s showing a gardener maintaining the ornamental fruit trees and topiaries.

Gilded bronze swans, by Rudolph Evans, survey the pool in front of the Italianate tea house, which was designed by William Welles Bosworth and built in 1908. Fanciful fountain spouts of sea-creatures were designed by F. M. L. Tonetti and manufactured by the Roman Bronze Works, Brooklyn, New York.

wide running down the center of the path is broken from place to place by small circular basins and water jets. Since 1908, underwater electric lights have illuminated the canal at night.

The teahouse in the inner garden was one of Mrs. John D. Rockefeller's favorite retreats. Its ceiling is painted with designs in the "grotesque" style Raphael used to decorate the Vatican Loggias and the loggias of the Villa Madama. Emil Siebern designed the relief panels and sculpted the marble figures of fairy children playing with a small faun in front of the teahouse pool. The room has its original 1910 chairs and day bed by William Baumgarten and Company; in the style of antique Roman furniture from Pompeii, they were probably designed by Bosworth. The carefully articulated classical or Italianate style of the teahouse, the most important place for shelter in the garden, successfully links the building to the gardens' overall classical theme.

A view of the south porch from the inner garden showing one of F.M.L. Tonetti's two groups of putti holding urns on the second-floor balcony.

When the garden was first completed, the topiaries, clipped into the shapes of animals and birds, were bought from the Yonkers nursery firm of Wadley and Smythe, who made at least two European buying trips to stock the gardens. The original color scheme of the flower borders of the inner garden was yellow and white, with dwarf pansies and snapdragons alternating spring and fall. From May through September several orange trees in tubs also stood at strategic places, along with palms and bay trees that Wadley and

Manipulator, 1954, by British artist, Reg Butler, sited by Nelson Rockefeller in front of a wall in the inner garden.

Smythe supplied. Wadley and Smythe staff shared the task of planting with Kykuit's head gardener and his men.

Nelson Rockefeller installed two swimming pools in the sunken areas, a deep one for adults and a shallow one for children (both have since been removed). Happy Rockefeller placed bird feeders around the garden to attract songbirds. Nelson also placed twentieth-century sculpture, including works by Aristide Maillol, Gaston Lachaise, Elie Nadelman, Reg Butler, Robert Adams, and Ezra Orion throughout the inner garden; Maillol's *Bather Putting up her Hair* (1930, after a small version of 1898) stands in the center of the two lawns (the pools of Nelson's day) on a pedestal that bridges the marble canal. Governor Rockefeller also placed two large Picasso vases in the teahouse, one in each corner, and he installed a soda fountain for his two young children.

Kykuit's landscaped gardens from the West terrace with views of the Hudson River and the Palisades beyond.

THE WEST PORCH

Kykuit was built around the spectacular views from the west porch. From here, the Tappan Zee, the Palisades, and the hills climbing toward Bear Mountain are all visible. Junior played a major role in the preservation of the Palisades and in the creation of Palisades Interstate Park. In good weather, the family used this covered porch as a living room, furnished it with carpets and wicker furniture, and took meals here.

The views from Kykuit inspired JDR. Soon after he bought the property, he built a surveying tower just south of this porch so that he could plan the exact position of the house and gardens. In his book, *Random Reminiscences of Men and Events*, JDR asserts his interest in landscape architecture and says that at Pocantico, "...all the old big trees were personal friends of mine." In the 1890s he employed the landscape architect Warren Manning of the Boston landscape firm of Olmsted, Olmsted & Eliot to draw preliminary landscape plans.

War Remembrance II, 1960-61, by Israeli-Rumanian sculptor, Sorel Etrog, placed atop the north wall of the west terrace. The roof of the rose garden pergola is visible on the right.

Bosworth, who took over from Manning in 1906, was equally inspired by the vista of the river and distant hills. His landscape designs here and elsewhere owe a debt to the work of William Kent, whose interiors had so influenced Codman. Kent approached nature as though it were a work of art. A painter before he became an architect, he had been much influenced by the baroque landscape paintings of Claude Lorrain and Nicholas Poussin. Many English parks were transformed using the principles of composition learned from these works, and Kent was the acknowledged master of creating outdoor settings to look like Old Master landscape paintings.

When Thomas Cole began to paint the Hudson Valley in the 1820s, he worked in the landscape tradition of Lorrain and Poussin and helped establish a taste for landscape and landscape painting in the United States. In 1870, the great Hudson River School painter Frederic Church, a

student of Cole, built Olana outside the city of Hudson with the help of architect Calvert Vaux. Olana, with its panoramic Hudson River view, was the ultimate model for the siting of the west porch at Kykuit.

The view from the porch into and across the gardens shows the striking impact that Nelson Rockefeller's sculpture collection has upon the landscape. He created a veritable outdoor sculpture museum, which considerably enhanced his father and grandfather's work to create a landscape of significant aesthetic value. Part of the three-thousand acre estate can also be seen from this porch. JDR and Junior laid out carriage trails through quiet glades, routes that provide alternate effects of grandeur and intimacy. Wishing to share the pleasure and inspiration they found here, the family has always kept many of the trails open to the public.

Corridor, about 1908, now one of the galleries. The long room boasts an original "Tile Arch System" ceiling, patented in the United States in 1885 by Catalan architect and builder, Rafael Guastavino, whose work is found in many buildings in New York City.

THE GALLERIES

At the bottom of the stairs leading from the main floor to the ground floor, the room on the left originally housed pipes for the Aeolian organ in the music room above. An original plan for the lower ground floor was to include a bowling alley, a popular feature in many large country houses of the time. The bowling alley was never installed in the space, which is now occupied by Galleries 1 and 2. Similarly, gallery 4 was originally a long corridor with a tiled floor where JDR's grandchildren could ride their bicycles.

Both of Nelson Rockefeller's parents were avid collectors, but by the time he came to live at Kykuit many of their paintings, prints and ceramics had been given to museums. Part of the remaining collection was displayed throughout the house. Kykuit was not designed to accommodate a collection of sculpture on the scale of the one Nelson had already amassed. His conversion of these ground-floor spaces into galleries

may have been suggested by his mother's earlier actions: at 10 West 54th Street, after her children had grown up, she had altered the nursery rooms to house her collection of folk and modern art.

On display here are more than one hundred works, mostly from the 1960s and 1970s and predominantly by

A series of eighteen tapestries after paintings by Picasso were commissioned by Nelson Rockefeller and woven in France by the Atelier J. de la Baume Dürrbach. Twelve are highlights of the art galleries at Kykuit.

American artists. In the gardens are an additional seventy twentieth-century sculptures Nelson placed there between 1963 and 1979. As a trustee of and major donor to the Museum of Modern Art for more than fifty years, Nelson Rockefeller was closely involved in the mission of MoMA's first director, Alfred H. Barr, Jr. to collect and interpret art of the modern age. As governor, Rockefeller created the New York State Council on the Arts, which became the prototype for the National Endowment for the Arts. Nelson was fascinated by art and architecture. He derived enormous pleasure from arranging his collections, often hanging the paintings himself. By the standards of most critics, he did it well.

Many of the works in the galleries at Kykuit were first shown in five of the six groundbreaking exhibitions held between 1942 and 1963 at the Museum of Modern Art, organized by Dorothy Miller, the museum's first curator of paintings: *Americans* (1942), *Fourteen Americans* (1946), *Fif-teen Americans* (1952), *Twelve Americans* (1956), *Sixteen Americans* (1959), and *Americans 1963*. These exhibitions were eagerly anticipated by the art world, and their influence reverberates in the history of 20th-century American art today. Included in the shows were works now at Kykuit by Bontecou, Higgins, Seley, Mallary, Hartigan, Lassaw, Lipton, Glarner, Marisol, Lytle, and Motherwell, among others.

Gallery 1

Alexander Calder, one of the most important American sculptors to work in Paris in the 1930s and 1940s, was the leader of the determined march of American artists toward abstract art. He also originated the modern concept of moving sculpture; his fine mobile *Black Sickles, Black Comma* was created in 1962. On the east wall hangs Robert Motherwell's *Granada: Elegy to the Spanish Republic II* (1949), which effectively represents the originality of New York's abstract expressionists.

Granada: Elegy to the Spanish Republic, II, 1949, by Robert Motherwell, one of the first in his epic series of more than 150 canvases on this same theme.

Shower Curtain, 1966, a plaster sculpture by George Segal, with Andy Warhol's portrait of Mrs. Nelson (Happy) Rockefeller in background, right.

Galleries 2 and 3

In these galleries are displayed the works of such well-known artists as Louise Nevelson, including *Transparent Sculpture #7* (1967–1968). Nevelson's small Plexiglas work uses abstract shapes similar to her large piece in the garden at Kykuit, *Atmosphere and Environment VI* (1967). Three tapestries by Alexander Calder on the south wall are a reminder of the artist's versatility in design and use of materials. Also in Gallery 3 originally was Calder's small stabile *Spiny* (1942), which Rockefeller bequeathed to the Museum of Modern Art. In 1966 he commissioned Calder to model *Large Spiny* on the thirty-inch original, and today that twelve-foot stabile stands in the northwest garden. Work by Marisol Escobar, Edgar Negret, Jorge Eielson, and Julio Alpuy reflect the considerable interest Rockefeller devel-

oped in the work of South American artists during his years of involvement in economic development on that continent.

Gallery 4

White plaster sculptures by George Segal, *Shower Curtain* (1966) and *Girl Holding Left Arm* (1973), command the first section of this long gallery that runs beneath the terraces. Portraits of Nelson Rockefeller and his wife Happy by Andy Warhol from 1967 and 1968 are installed at the mid-point. Grace Hartigan's 1956 *City Life*, illustrating a vibrant city scene, is paired with Louise Kruger's *Bicycle Rider*.

The vaulted and tiled ceilings in galleries 4 and 5, and in the Grotto under the Temple of Venus, were designed and manufactured by the Guastavino Fireproof Construction Company, founded in 1889 by Rafael Guastivino. An émi-

Interior with Girl Drawing, one of the twelve Picasso tapestries hanging at Kykuit. Each tapestry, commissioned by Nelson Rockefeller, was based on a Picasso painting.

gré from Barcelona, Spain, Guastivino developed a unique system of vaulting, expressed in longer spans of space with a low rise, made possible by the light weight of the tiles and the cohesive strength of the mortar. Rafael Guastivino patented this construction method, which he had adapted from the catalan vault, a centuries-old fire-proofing method.

Gallery 5

The last gallery explodes with an exuberance of color in the large tapestries, after paintings by Picasso, each commissioned by Nelson Rockefeller with the permission of the artist and woven between 1958 and 1975. The complete series numbered eighteen, of which fifteen remain at Pocantico. All were woven by Mme J. de la Baume Dürrbach and her studio in the south of France. The first of the series, after the painting, *Guernica*, (June 1937), was painted for the Spanish Government building at the Paris World's Fair; it was Picasso's strong response to the destruction of a Basque town in April of that year. The painting traveled extensively until 1956, then remained at the Museum of Modern Art until 1981, when it was returned to Spain. The tapestry of *Guernica* remains in a family collection and currently hangs at the United Nations.

A number of the periods of Picasso's work are surveyed in the tapestry collection; the earliest Picasso composition at Kykuit (and the final tapestry commission in 1975) is after *Girl with Mandolin* (1910), the early cubist composition owned by Nelson Rockefeller and bequeathed to MoMA. Unlike the other tapestries that are woven of wool, *Girl with Mandolin* is woven with silk, making the subtle colors of the fragmented, semi-geometric shapes seem to shimmer.

The bold simplicity and flat forms of *Harlequin* (1915) and *Three Musicians* (1921) are typical of synthetic cubism. In *Pitcher and Bowl of Fruit* (1931), the forms remain flat, but curve and are bordered by bold black lines that refer to stained glass compositions. In *Girls with Toy Boat* (1937), the calm of the beach scene is disturbed by a large menacing head looming on the horizon, reflecting the disquiet of the times.

In *Night Fishing at Antibes* (1939), the ordinary becomes alarming. Two girls watch at a dock with bicycle and ice cream, as bright lights, intended to bring fish to the surface, explode in the night sky, one emitting a blood red

Gallery 5 tapestries. These hangings are based on Picasso's paintings and were woven in France, under his supervision, by Jacqueline de la Baume Dürrbach. Mme. Dürrbach lived and worked at Cavalaire in the south of France, not far from where Picasso lived. The tapestries at Kykuit are from a group of eighteen, commissioned by Nelson Rockefeller between about 1955 and 1974.

smoke. As one figure spears a flounder, another dives, his expression one of alarm.

For the creation of each tapestry, a detailed process was followed carefully. Transparencies accompanied by color charts and yarns matched to the original paintings were sent to the weaver. A cartoon of the composition (a pattern the size of the tapestry) was created and placed beneath the warp of the loom as a template for the weaver to follow. In all but one case, permission was granted for editions of

three. Photographs of authentication were signed by Picasso.

Nelson Rockefeller also exhibited some of these bold, striking tapestry compositions in the Executive Mansion in Albany to encourage the understanding and appreciation of modern art, a mission very important to him. Portable, less fragile, and less costly than the paintings, these tapestries were installed, too, in some of the more unconventional spaces of the family's homes including the boat house gallery in Maine.

THE GARDENS AND LANDSCAPE

*I*n 1906, as the construction of Kykuit had reached the first floor, Junior hired William Welles Bosworth to plan the formal gardens. Bosworth, like Junior a native of Ohio, had received his degree in architecture from the Massachusetts Institute of Technology in 1889 and had worked for the landscape architect Frederick Law Olmsted. While traveling in Europe between 1899 and 1901, Bosworth attended the École des Beaux-Arts in Paris and there met Chester Aldrich, later hired to design the first stage of the house at Kykuit.

Bosworth's Kykuit garden, including the entrance façade, is considered his best work in the United States, where he practiced until the end of World War I. In 1913, with Kykuit virtually complete, Junior hired Bosworth to design a substantial eight-story townhouse (now demolished) at 10 West 54th Street in New York City, next door to his parents' home. Beginning in 1926, as general secretary of the French-American Committee for the Restoration of Historic Monuments, Bosworth supervised the restoration of the palaces of Versailles and Fontainebleau and the cathedrals at Rheims and Chartres, projects all funded in large measure by Junior.

In 1905, the year before Bosworth began to work at Kykuit, Edith Wharton published *Italian Villas and Their Gardens*, with illustrations by the well-known artist Maxfield Parrish. Like *The Decoration of Houses*, this book became a key source on contemporary high style and a significant statement of the renewed interest in classical design. Just as Kykuit's interiors show this influence, the gardens reflect this aesthetic as well.

American gardens of the early twentieth century were largely based on two principles in which Bosworth and other American architects had been drilled at the École des Beaux-Arts. One principle dictated that outdoor spaces be arranged in clear, orderly ways, positioned either along a main sight line (usually a walking path) or so as to terminate at a focal point such as a sculpture or a beautiful view. The second principle dictated the use of strong vertical planes, such as evergreen hedges, shrub borders, or stone walls, to give definition to the outdoors. The gardens closest to the house were to be geometric and rectilinear. The outer reaches of the property were to be parkland. As his model for Kykuit, Bosworth consciously took Italian gardens, which he termed "the origin of all subsequent garden tradition." Terraces in particular, he noted were "so preferred by Italians for gardens on a hilltop site with the ground falling steeply away towards the view;" Kykuit's similar topography—which Bosworth said resembled "an inverted oyster shell, flat only at the top and hardly flat there"— recommended the Italian model even more strongly.

Except for the 1913 extension of the entrance forecourt, the gardens Bosworth planned in 1906 are essentially what exist today—the inner garden with the brook garden and Temple of Venus beyond, the west terraces with the swimming pool, and the semicircular rose garden. Trees that have died have been carefully and appropriately

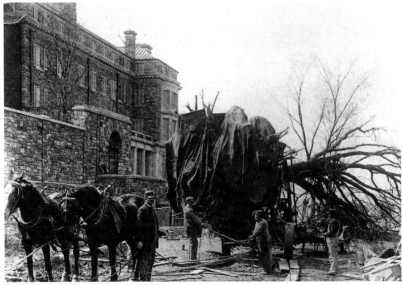

Full-grown tree being brought to the garden around the rebuilt house, 1913 or 1914, by Hicks Nurseries of Westbury, Long Island.

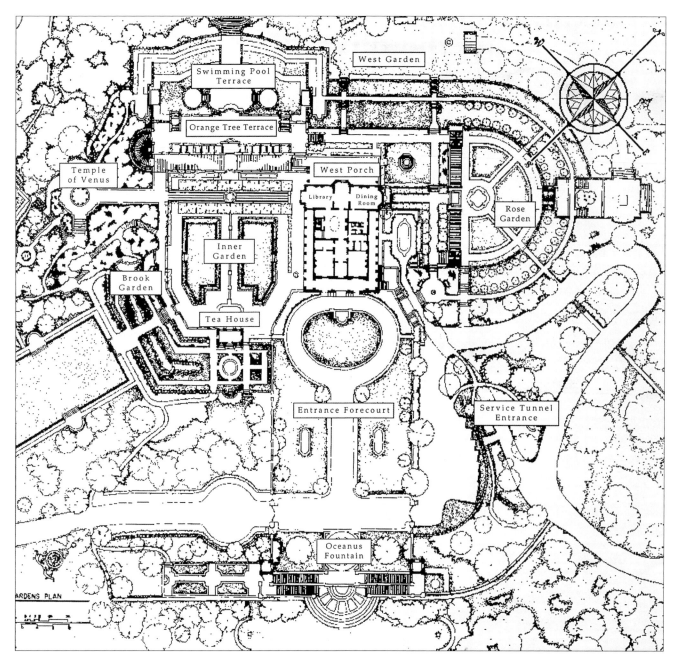

Labels within the image:
Swimming Pool Terrace
Orange Tree Terrace
West Garden
Temple of Venus
West Porch
Library
Dining Room
Rose Garden
Inner Garden
Brook Garden
Tea House
Entrance Forecourt
Service Tunnel Entrance
Oceanus Fountain
ARDENS PLAN

Garden plan with the house in the center. Although the Hudson River is located about two miles west of Kykuit, there are magnificent views of the river and up and down the Valley from the west-side terraces and paths.

replaced while others have matured, but the architectural framework of the gardens is still clearly visible. Bosworth's use throughout the garden of roughly cut stones and boulders is consistent with the traditional rustic aesthetic of a country garden; a city garden would have demanded finely cut stonework. Bosworth's goal was both to maintain and enhance the river view and to create an accessible garden with many and varied walks on which visitors and family might enjoy nature transformed. Because the family intended the place principally as a spring and fall retreat (JDR continued to spend summers at Forest Hill, and Junior was

usually in Maine), Kykuit had no summer flower garden; spring bulbs and blossoms and fall foliage provided color. In Nelson's time, when the family came to Kykuit on early summer weekends, a more colorful planting plan was developed for the brook garden.

In the overall plan, the river view from the west porch came first. Bosworth intended to transform this view into a panorama comparable to the paintings of Thomas Cole or Frederic Church. Any intrusions into the composition, including some old roads, were moved or obliterated. The Kykuit gardens required a difficult fusion between the demands of a conventional Beaux-Arts garden plan, with long vistas and paths leading away from the house, often on all four points of the compass, and the English idea of a house surrounded by rolling landscape. To achieve this marriage, Bosworth broke one of the traditional axes of the Beaux-Arts or Italian garden, the one that usually ran from the formal approach to a house through the building and into the garden for a considerable distance. Bosworth's east entrance to the house is along an axis that continues due west through the hall, music room, and alcove room but is abruptly terminated by the west porch so that the Hudson River landscape can take over as the principal view. The east/west axis is then shifted a hundred feet to the south to be on line with the Italianate tea house and the lower west terraces. The second or north/south axis runs unbroken through the house with long garden vistas. However, it is designed off-center so that it passes not through the middle of the building but through the west suite of family rooms, the library and dining room. Thus, from these rooms two impressive garden vistas present themselves—south to the Temple of Venus and north to the semicircular rose garden with its maze (no longer extant) and loggia.

Bosworth's creation is the core of a great estate or "family seat" and is today one of the best and grandest surviving Beaux-Arts gardens in the United States. Traditionally gardens are a means of self-cultivation and an expression of a garden owner's most deeply-held values. For both JDR and Junior this meant that the gardens must emphasize order and rationality, values that are part and parcel of traditions stretching back to the Italian Renaissance and rooted in antiquity.

THE MAIN FAÇADE AND ENTRANCE FORECOURT

The Kykuit entrance is the quintessential "American Renaissance" ensemble, designed to capture the grand traditions of classical history. The 1913 façade is in the style of the well-known Italian Renaissance villas by Andrea Palladio. Bosworth used the pediment to reference the architecture of Roman antiquity, just as Palladio had four hundred years earlier and as William Kent had done in eighteenth-century England. The classical emblems of spring, summer, and fall and of architecture, painting, and music around the central windows of the second and third floors were carved by F. M. L. Tonetti, who also sculpted the flanking vases with putti holding up baskets. The bronze work balconies and the entrance canopy, also designed within the classical vocabulary, were supplied by Tiffany Studios in New York City.

The doubling of the forecourt's length to complement

East forecourt in 1913, with the new entrance façade under construction and preparations being made for the installation of the Oceanus fountain.

The grand stairway descends from the Oceanus fountain to the stone mosaic of zodiac signs for spring, summer, and fall. The zodiac signs represented at Kykuit refer to the months that the Rockefeller family lived on the estate, during both Senior's and Junior's times.

Adam and Eve sculpture and fountain, George Gray Barnard, 1923, with signs of the zodiac radiating outward. To the right is a detail of the sign of Virgo, August 22–September 23.

From the front porch to the east, the Oceanus fountain after Giambologna is set at the end of the forecourt and a double row of honey locust trees. The main figure faces west toward the Hudson River, symbolically linking the rivers of the old world with a great American river.

the façade created an impressive entrance framed by walls and magnificent wrought-iron gates. Designed by Bosworth according to European prototypes, they were made by W. H. Jackson Company of New York. This enclosure incorporates four fountains, the largest of which is the nearly thirty-foot Oceanus group, placed to catch the eye both from the driver's approach through the entrance gates and from the house itself. In Roman mythology, Oceanus was the father of the river gods as well as a symbol of the universal power of water and thus of the origin of all things. In his privately printed 1919 book on the gardens, Bosworth wrote that the fountain's three lower figures may represent three rivers—the Nile, the Euphrates, and the Ganges. Im-

plicitly, the fountain associates the Hudson, one of America's most important waterways, with the great rivers of the old world. Bosworth wanted visitors to pass from a view of the fountain "directly to the west porch where the full effect of the magnificent view of the river and distant mountains is disclosed."

The Italian Renaissance prototype for the Kykuit Oceanus was a figure commissioned from the sculptor Giambologna about 1565 as the central feature of the Boboli Gardens at the Pitti Palace in Florence. Edith Wharton used illustrations of the fountain in her *Italian Villas and Their Gardens* to show the epitome of the concept of focus in a classical garden. The Kykuit Oceanus was made in Italy in

A closer view of the Oceanus fountain showing two of the three river gods surrounding the large central figure of Oceanus.

BELOW: The Oceanus fountain under construction. The figure standing mid-way up is thought to be William Welles Bosworth, the Beaux-Arts architect who designed the landscape and gardens at Kykuit. Bosworth also conceived the idea of lengthening the forecourt and placing the monumental fountain at its east end.

1913; the granite bowl was produced on Crotch Island, near Stonington, Maine, and shipped in June 1914. The bowl, twenty feet in diameter and weighing thirty-five tons, arrived in North Tarrytown by water and was hauled up Beekman Avenue and Bedford Road from the dock on a heavy truck running over planks to protect the surfaces of the roads. No damage occurred, though the town required a $50,000 personal bond from JDR against the possibility. Large orange trees in wooden tubs, or "caisses de Versailles," were placed around the fountain during frost-free months; in winter these trees were kept in Bosworth's specially built orangerie near the park entrance. Orange trees were on the property until the early 1980s when the family donated them to various botanical gardens. The Hicks Nursery of Westbury, Long Island was among those who were contracted with to provide the full-grown trees for the forecourt, to create the impression of a home that had been there for generations.

THE MORNING GARDEN

The morning garden was designed to be used, but also to be seen from the balcony of the tea house. This calm and sequestered area, which features a central, circular pool with fountainhead by F. M. L. Tonetti, would have been viewed to best advantage from above, creating an excellent focus from the tea house windows. The bronze figure of Victory, which rises above the morning garden, was described by Bosworth as "a facsimile of the one from Pompeii now in the Naples Museum." Its supporting column was bought by Junior from the estate of the architect Stanford White. In the south-facing wall of the morning garden is set a relief roundel of an eagle, described by Bosworth as coming from a church in Venice. Today, a bronze cast copy replaces the original deteriorated piece.

The morning garden with its central fountain; the fountainhead was designed by F. M. L. Tonetti. Viewed from the tea house, a favorite place of Laura Spelman Rockefeller, this garden room provides a transition space from the formality of the entrance forecourt and serves as an entrance to the brook garden beyond.

THE BROOK GARDEN

Rock was virtually all there was on top of Kykuit hill when the garden began; certainly there was no water; so the brook had to be created. The brook garden reflected the focus of interest in Asian plants and gardens during the late-nineteenth and early-twentieth centuries. Plant exploration was in its heyday in the mid-1800s, and many species were imported into America, particularly from Japan. The brook garden was planted with several weeping cherry trees, *Prunus subhirtella pendula,* which remain a feature of the spring garden at Kykuit. The Japanese bronze lanterns, here since 1908,

The brook garden, reflecting the Asian influence popular at the turn of the twentieth century. This garden is especially lovely in spring, when the weeping Japanese Higan cherry trees are in full flower. The Japanese bronze lanterns, added in 1908, enhance the Asian reference.

OPPOSITE: Nelson Rockefeller continued the Asian theme when he added *Jubilee,* 1965, by the Japanese artist, Masayuki Nagare and, on the pedestal on the right side of the brook that runs through the center of the garden, *Black Sun,* 1960–63, by Japanese-American sculptor, Isamu Noguchi.

add to the Asian reference, which Nelson further strengthened by the addition of sculpture by the Japanese artist Masayuki Nagare and the Japanese-American Isamu Noguchi.

THE TEMPLE OF VENUS

Located south of the linden allée, the Temple of Venus is a prominent feature just outside the boundary of the inner garden (the inner garden is discussed earlier in the text). Viewed from the garden or from the house, the Temple of Venus is the major architectural feature of the south terraces. It was designed by Bosworth to house the Venus sculpture, a nineteenth-century replica of a lost original by the Greek sculptor Praxiteles. The sculpture and the temple emphasize the classical origins of the house and garden design.

The Temple of Venus shown in Autumn. The temple, placed within a small grove of American dogwood, *Cornus florida*, and Japanese dogwood, *Cornus kousa*, plays a central role in the garden plan. It is situated in the site line of the French doors to the library, perhaps as a reference to classical art and learning. The Aphrodite sculpture is set on a revolving pedestal.

LEFT: The classic beauty of the marble Aphrodite, set against the detailed temple ceiling.

OPPOSITE: The linden allée, which forms the west boundary of the inner garden. The Temple of Venus is just beyond the inner garden to the south. A Moorish fountain, foreground, features a bronze fountainhead of Orpheus by F. M. L. Tonetti.

51

Grotto. Located directly beneath the Temple of Venus, this large, interior grotto is a circular room of rough-cut stone. It houses sculptures by Emil Siebern, who worked at Kykuit between 1909 and 1914, and features a Guastavino tile ceiling and Moravian tile floors. Nelson Rockefeller added the *Futuristic Flowers* by Italian artist, Giacomo Balla, to complement the exotic atmosphere of the room.

THE GROTTO

Stairs descend from the classical temple to the Grotto beneath, a magical space, a folly in the tradition of Italian gardens, providing a cool refuge on the hottest of summer days. Nymphs and a satyr with cymbals, bronzes by Emil Siebern, inhabit the space, each within a pool where once the gentle splash of water enhanced the cool reserve. The walls are of sandstone blocks and there are stalactites, imported from caves in Genoa that are also used throughout the gardens. Carved sandstone heads, antique forms recalling masks for the Roman theater, top each of the eight columns. The floor is paved with Moravian tiles, among the first designs produced by Henry Mercer's tileworks in Doylestown, Pennsylvania. Icicle-form lights of frosted glass, designed by Bosworth and made by Tiffany Furnaces, cast a cool green light. The potted palms that once filled the space have been replaced by the sculptures of *Futuristic Flowers* by Giacomo Balla.

Early drawings and letters indicate that the Grotto was first designed with a domed ceiling, a Guastavino structure and tiles; a large urn was placed at its center. In 1916 with the arrival of the Aphrodite sculpture and its base for the Temple of Venus above, JDR, Jr. brought back the engineers to determine whether the ceiling was strong enough to support the additional weight. Thompson & Starrett expressed concern that the dome of the grotto ceiling was already overburdened by the temple itself, a much more substantial structure than originally planned, with its seven marble columns and elaborate roof. They called for the addition of a central column, with radiating support bands within which Guastavino adapted their arch system.

One of eight sandstone heads carved for the top of each column in the grotto.

One of Balla's *Futuristic Flowers*, designed about 1919, probably as part of a stage set. This edition dates from the 1960s.

Detail of one of the grotto's Moravian floor tiles, made at Henry Chapman Mercer's tileworks in Doylestown, Pennsylvania.

Reclining Woman, one of three figures in the grotto by sculptor, Emil Siebern.

1931, had been commissioned for a garden in the south of France where it was surrounded by a dramatic landscape. That setting inspired the raised position of this later bronze version, which overlooks the river scenery. *Song of the Vowels* was based on an ancient Egyptian prayer composed only of vowels and sung to subdue the powerful and sometimes destructive forces of nature. The sculpture shows two figures playing harps as if accompanying the song.

Song of the Vowels by Jacques Lipchitz, 1931–32. Sited on the orange tree terrace in 1972 by Nelson Rockefeller, this monumental sculpture, cast in 1952–53, overlooks the Hudson River and the Palisades.

THE ORANGE TREE TERRACE

All of Kykuit's terraces were created out of a rocky hillside using dynamite, machinery, and hard labor. Topsoil was brought in from other parts of the estate to create level surfaces where there had been none. In old Italian gardens, the terrace above or below the level of the flower garden close to the house was traditionally planted with fruit trees. At Kykuit, Bosworth designed this terrace, below the level of the main rooms and in the inner garden, for the display of citrus trees. Between 1908 and 1980 eight large orange trees stood here in tubs during the frost-free months. The metal balustrade, designed by Bosworth with bronze vines and grapes (as part of the fruit theme of the terrace), were made by the Tiffany Studios, which also made the lanterns of Bosworth's design.

In the wall niche, lined with stalactites and stalagmites brought from Italy, is Karl Bitter's *Girl with a Goose* (1914), commissioned by Bosworth and Junior for this location. Bitter had a large factory for the production of decorative sculpture, mostly for public buildings but also for large houses and gardens.

Nelson Rockefeller placed Jacques Lipchitz's bronze sculpture *Song of the Vowels* (1953) here in 1972. The first casting of this work by Lipchitz, in

Karl Bitter's *The Goose Girl*, 1914. Set in a niche surrounded by stalagmites and stalactites brought from Italy, *The Goose Girl* was commissioned by John D. Rockefeller, Jr. specifically for this location.

The swimming pool terrace looking up toward the house with the orange tree terrace above. On the left in the distance is *Triangular Surface in Space,* 1962, by Max Bill, placed by Nelson Rockefeller at the west end of the rose garden pergola.

THE SWIMMING POOL TERRACE

This terrace features three pools, all lined with circular patterns of black and white pebbles imported from Italy. The largest of the pools, in the center, was intended for swimming. Its deep end is at the west, and steps drop down into it at the north and south ends. JDR's grandchildren swam here. Overflow from the pool pours down spillways, spanned by small bridges of rustic stone covered with clematis into circular pools at either side. The swimming pool itself is fed from a stalactite grotto set into the wall below the orange tree terrace. On the outer edge of the pool is *Nuclear Energy* by British sculptor Henry Moore, the larger version of which was commissioned by the University of Chicago to mark the twenty-fifth anniversary of the first controlled release of nuclear energy in 1942. This maquette, at four feet high a third of the size of the original, is one of the artist's models for the final sculpture.

The terrace was originally shaded by six large elm trees that survived until the early 1980s, when they were

Surveying tower set above the construction area of the orange tree and swimming pool terraces, September 1907.

replaced by honey locusts. The two latticework summer houses were once flanked by large jasmine trees imported from England. Below the summer house, at the terrace's south end, is an octagonal "bandstand."

55

Knife-Edge, Two Piece, 1965–66. Nelson Rockefeller sited this monumental sculpture by Henry Moore at the south end of the gardens, adjacent to the golf course. In autumn, the polished bronze reflects the burnished tones of the fall foliage.

THE WEST GARDEN

The terraces continue down the Kykuit hillside to include a putting green laid out in 1901 as part of what is now a nine-hole reversible golf course. Around the green stand four sculptures Nelson Rockefeller placed here in the 1960s and 1970s—Louise Nevelson's *Atmosphere and Environment VI* (1967); Gaston Lachaise's *Man* (ca. 1935); *Horse* (1951) by Marino Marini; and Aristide Maillol's *Night* (1905). Beyond the copper beach hedge is Alexander Calder's stabile *Large Spiny* (1966), which Nelson Rockefeller commissioned for this site; James Rosati's *Lippincott II* (1969); Eduardo Paolozzi's *Akapotic Rose* (1965); and one of Henry Moore's masterpieces, *Knife-Edge, Two Piece* (1965).

Seen from above, the west garden and putting green command striking views of the Hudson River. The central, large figure on the east side of the putting green is *Man*, by Gaston Lachaise, 1930–35; in the distance is Aristide Maillol's *Night*, 1902–09.

THE ROSE GARDEN

Bosworth designed the semicircular rose garden as the principal feature of the north terraces. With its colonnade arbor and Renaissance revival fountain, the garden's symmetry is distinctly classical. The cultivation of roses has been universal for centuries. Modern rose culture dates from the fifteenth and sixteenth centuries when ever-blooming and monthly roses were imported from Asia to Europe in East India Company ships. Renaissance poets wrote about roses, and in the United States gentlemen on country estates often kept specimen rose gardens to indulge an interest in natural science and genetics, as well as to reference these European traditions. In the original design, a maze, which no longer survives, also reflected the influence of these traditions, as mazes had been much used in courtly landscapes of the Renaissance. Because hybrid tea roses flower in the late spring and again in the fall, they were thought particularly appropriate for Kykuit, which was used mostly during those seasons.

Kykuit's rose garden, designed by William Welles Bosworth as the principal feature of the north terraces. In its semi-circular form, with its colonnade arbors and Renaissance-revival fountain, this garden is typical of Beaux-Arts design. The fountain, a replica of one at the Boboli gardens in Florence, is topped by a carved stone figure based on a Donatello sculpture.

Examples of Moravian tiles that form the floor of the rose garden pergola. These tiles, as well as those in the grotto, were manufactured at Henry Chapman Mercer's tileworks in Doylestown, Pennsyvania. The use of the tiles as decorative features at Kykuit reflects the influence of the arts and crafts movement in America in the early 1900s.

THE ORANGERIE

Drawing of the Orangerie, published in 1907.

Like all of the original garden buildings, the orangerie (whose interior is not on the tour) was designed by Bosworth. It was constructed during the summer of 1908 at great speed so that the recently arrived orange trees, bay trees, jasmines, and other non-hardy plants could be housed before the fall frost. Most of the original ornamental sweet-smelling trees were imported from England, France, and Holland; many were brought here as mature specimens. The tall, arched windows place the orangerie firmly in the European tradition for such structures. It once had an elaborate winter heating system, but since the early 1980s, when the collection of ornamental trees was donated to botanical gardens, the structure ceased to be used and thus is no longer heated.

Interior of the Orangerie in winter, about 1915.

THE GARDEN'S ENDURING ROLE

The gardens at Kykuit gracefully incorporate its multiple influences: the classical vision of William Welles Bosworth, the focus of JDR on landscape pleasures and of JDR, Jr. on creating a setting amenable to and worthy of his father, and the exuberant inspiration of Nelson Rockefeller, who enriched the garden rooms with his twentieth-century sculpture collection. In his self-published book on the gardens of Kykuit, Bosworth explores his own perceptions of the design, and in doing so he reveals the decidedly modern approach that has allowed these gardens to maintain their brilliance over the course of almost one hundred years:

"Here one may stroll for a mile or more along paths within easy call of the house, winding in and out through shaded walks or sunny terraces. Here are tea houses and pavilions, enclosed and open, to suit all seasons, weathers, or time of day. Just as one's collection of books, pictures, and music respond to the varying moods and temperaments of a family, so do the diversified features of this garden."

Entrance to the garage of the coach barn with its
1918 Crane Simplex touring car, which John D.
Rockefeller, Jr. used regularly around the estate.

THE COACH BARN

Horses for carriages and for riding have long held a special place in the lives of men and women who had the leisure to enjoy them. The horse's strength, speed, and courage symbolized the status of the owner. During his early years in Cleveland and after he came to New York, John D. Rockefeller drove carriages for sport and raced fine horses both singly and in pairs. At the end of the nineteenth century, when coaching became fashionable, he also practiced the difficult sport of driving four-in-hand. JDR initiated the building of extensive bridle paths and drives throughout the estate, beginning soon after he acquired the property. Sometimes he did the surveying himself, and he was always directly involved in planning the routes and in creating picturesque vistas. Today the Coach Barn can be seen within its original context, set in parkland, and with much of its collection intact. Some carriages have been added, and the horses that once were here are now absent. Apart from these changes, the interiors have changed little since John D. Rockefeller, Jr. died in 1960.

The coach barn stands on the site of the original Parsons-Wentworth stables and carriage house, which burned in 1895, seven years before that house itself was destroyed by fire in 1902. New York architects York and Sawyer designed this coach barn in 1901 and completed it in 1902; Kykuit architects Delano and Aldrich modified it in 1907. The building today is, like the rest of the grounds at Kykuit, largely the work of Bosworth. By 1916, he had changed the main façade, with its clock tower and rustic stonework, and refigured the interiors to accommodate automobiles. The original carriage room on the west side

Runabout or governess cart with four of Junior and Abby's six children, Laurance, Babs, Nelson, and JDR 3rd, spring 1911.

was converted to an automobile garage. On the east side, what had originally been stables became a combined carriage room and stable for eleven horses. Today sixteen horse-drawn vehicles are housed here, and in the garage there are thirteen vintage automobiles once used by members of the Rockefeller family.

The Carriages

The carriage industry in America developed rapidly between about 1840 and 1860. Centered in New York, carriage makers produced increasingly elaborate pleasure vehicles until the turn of the century, when automobiles began to replace them. Not all the manufacturers of the vehicles in the collection are known, but five carry labels of New York City makers, and two were made in Glens Falls, New York. The New York City vehicles include the road coach, used for four-in-hand driving, made by A.T. Demarest on East 13th Street in 1892, and the basket runabout, or governess cart, bought from Van Tassel and Kearney. The two buckboards, or surreys, were made in Glens Falls. They were designed for long country drives, and tradition holds that Abby Aldrich Rockefeller drove them.

The Automobiles

The fact that the gas-powered automobile so quickly eclipsed the horse-drawn carriage not only revolutionized American life but ensured the continued profitability of Standard Oil. Originally, petroleum had been refined into

Vehicle for children learning to drive or for fun around the park about 1915.

The carriage room of the coach barn today, showing the original hanging lamps with Vaseline glass globes.

kerosene, which replaced lard and whale oils as the illuminant of choice in America until the discovery and commercial success of electricity in the last two decades of the nineteenth century. Just as electricity promised to make kerosene obsolete, the internal combustion engine provided a new and seemingly infinite market for refined petroleum.

The earliest car in the collection is a 1907 Ford Model S. The 1916 Detroit Electric continued to be used locally through the time of gas rationing during World War II. The 1918 Crane Simplex touring car has a body by Brew-

ster, which strongly resembles that of a carriage; many early automobile makers had been carriage makers only a few decades earlier. Junior used the Crane Simplex regularly around the estate. The 1939 Cadillac convertible was also his; there are many photographs of Junior using it at Colonial Williamsburg. Also garaged here are Nelson Rockefeller's 1959 Chrysler limousine with its "Governor" license plates and the 1966 Datsun, purchased from the New York World's Fair.

Lippincott II, 1965–69, by James Rosati, framed by sugar maple trees and set on a path below the rose garden, with views of the Hudson River visible through the trees.

OPPOSITE: Against a background of mugo pine and white pine, Pablo Picasso's *The Bathers*, 1956–57, was sited by Governor Rockefeller just outside the low wall of the brook garden and adjacent to the former tennis court.

NELSON ROCKEFELLER'S
SCULPTURE COLLECTION

*O*f the hundreds of works of art Nelson Rockefeller collected, it was sculpture to which he was most drawn. Between 1935 and the late 1970s, he assembled an extensive collection, and while Gov. Rockefeller made major gifts from his fine arts collection to museums, often anonymously, his finest sculptures, 120 objects, remain at Kykuit.

From both a historical and aesthetic point of view and because of the range and completeness of the collection, these sculptures are the most important part of the art collections at Kykuit. The collection includes works by those sculptors in Europe and the United States who are widely thought to have created some of the most original art of the twentieth century—Pablo Picasso, Constantin Brancusi, Jean Arp, Alexander Calder, Alberto Giacometti, Henry Moore, Isamu Noguchi, Louise Nevelson, and David Smith.

Nelson began to acquire many of these works after World War II, when most collectors remained preoccupied with painting, and he assembled works by both well-known and little-known sculptors; in the 1950s, when he purchased works by such sculptors as David Smith and Reg Butler, they were relatively obscure.

Governor Rockefeller once said, "I am more drawn to the plastic, three-dimensional, than to pure line and color. I seriously considered being an architect when I was in college; perhaps my love for sculpture is related to my forgotten vocation." His mother stimulated his interest in art in 1929, when he was still a student at Dartmouth College, by taking Nelson to the avant-garde galleries in downtown Manhattan. "If you start to cultivate your taste and eye so young," she once wrote to Nelson, "you ought to be very good at it by the time you can afford to collect... Art is one

At the west end of the inner garden, an Etruscan oil jar, one of a pair, provides a focal point along the low wall. Providing a feast for the eyes, David Smith's *Banquet*, 1951, is sited atop a wall of the west terrace.

of the great resources of my life. I believe that it not only enriches the spiritual life, but that it makes one more sane and sympathetic, more observant and understanding, regardless of whatever age it springs from, whatever subject it represents."

Although his mother inspired Nelson to collect, two other people were important influences on him—Alfred H. Barr, Jr., who became the first director of the Museum of Modern Art in 1929 at the age of twenty-seven, and Dorothy Miller, the museum's first curator of paintings. "From the start," Nelson wrote in 1969, "Alfred and Dorothy set standards, as those of us who shared their interests felt our way in these innovations of expression. They not only helped us to understand, but they gave us courage to make our own decisions." Rene d'Harnoncourt, another director of MoMA, was also one of Nelson's close advisors. It therefore comes as no surprise that Gov. Rockefeller's twentieth-century sculpture collection is quite complementary to that of the Museum of Modern Art's.

Sculpture often looks best on a site framed by architecture and a place with space around it; garden settings are particularly ideal because they are intentionally created as spaces in which people experience and relate to the natural world and seek solace and renewal. At Kykuit, the house acts as a visual anchor for the collection of sculpture around it; visitors walk through various three-dimensional spaces—enclosed gardens, terraces at different levels whose walls and hedges create volume, and garden pavilions and gazebos. Sculpture is fundamentally a physical presence; it creates a physical and psychological impression. In paintings, volume is only described on the surface of the canvas. Viewers cannot enter a painting as they can the space of a sculpture. Indeed, the presence of three-dimensional art can enliven the space around it. Bosworth certainly envisioned sculpture in this role when he created the Kykuit gardens, directly based on European Renaissance models in which sculpture was integral to the design.

Although Bosworth was enamored of the way sculpture was used in Italian gardens, it was Nelson who actually realized the concept at Kykuit. In the 1960s, when he began to place twentieth-century pieces around the grounds, he both continued a western tradition and was part of a movement that pioneered the sculpture garden in the United States. Moreover, most of his works were abstract, avant garde, modern, a remarkable departure from the classical legacy of the gardens themselves.

At the end of the rose garden pergola, *Triangular Surface in Space*, 1962, by Max Bill, directs attention to the view of the Hudson River and the Palisades beyond.

BELOW: Sited just below the swimming pool terrace, *Dans la Nuit*, 1935, by Gaston Lachaise, is placed in front of a yew hedge.

OPPOSITE: Alexander Calder's *Large Spiny*, 1966, commissioned by Nelson Rockefeller. A larger version of a similar piece from 1942, also owned by Governor Rockefeller and now in the collection of the Museum of Modern Art, this painted metal work reflects Calder's use of circus themes with shapes that are reminiscent of whimsical animals, perhaps giraffes.

BIOGRAPHIES

JOHN D. ROCKEFELLER
(1839–1937)

John D. Rockefeller was born in upstate New York on a farm not far from Binghamton in the southern tier, a landscape of hills that he dearly loved. He was a descendant of Johann Peter Rockefeller, who arrived in North America from the German Palatinate in 1723. JDR's father, William Avery Rockefeller, was a trader dealing in such commodities as salt and timber. He married Eliza Davison in 1830, and John Davison Rockefeller was the couple's second child and eldest son.

By the time he was a teenager, JDR had moved with his family to Cleveland, Ohio, where he was baptized at Erie Street Baptist Church. He began in business at the age of sixteen as a clerk accountant for two Cleveland wholesale and shipping merchants. In 1858, JDR and a partner began their own company, and by 1863 Rockefeller entered the oil refinery business. Petroleum had been discovered in Pennsylvania only four years earlier, and Cleveland, one of the early centers of oil refining, was on the brink of vast industrial expansion. In March 1864, Rockefeller married Laura Spelman, a young Cleveland woman with a strong political and religious background; her parents were staunch abolitionists and active in the Underground Railroad. In 1884, Spelman Seminary in Atlanta, for African American women, was named in honor of her parents; JDR provided substantial financial support to the institution.

By 1870, when Rockefeller and his partners incorporated themselves as the Standard Oil Company, their refinery was producing more than fifteen hundred barrels of kerosene a day, destined for street and indoor lamps all over the country. Even before the gasoline engine opened up a completely new and almost limitless demand for refined petroleum, Standard Oil and its competitors supplied a huge market. At the end of the decade, Standard Oil had bought out or merged with twenty-two of its twenty-five Cleveland competitors, and it produced 33 million of the 36 million barrels of oil then produced in the United States.

By 1884, when JDR moved to New York City, Standard Oil was well on its way to becoming one of the largest corporations of its day, and he was soon to become one of the wealthiest men in the world. Throughout, he remained a deeply religious man, worshipping all his life within the Baptist faith in which he had been reared. His mother, whose favorite motto was "willful waste makes woeful want," instilled in her son a veneration for work and a profound sense of charitable obligation.

Charity was an essential part of JDR's life from his youth; a strong religious impulse underlay and always informed his giving. Even when the affairs of Standard Oil demanded nearly his full attention, JDR spent more and more time on philanthropy. By his death in 1937 at the age

John D. Rockefeller with his son Junior (standing), his daughter-in-law Abby Aldrich Rockefeller, and his six grandchildren, John 3rd, David, Babs, Winthrop, Nelson, and Laurance, about 1918.

OPPOSITE: John D. Rockefeller and John D. Rockefeller, Jr. about 1920.

of ninety-seven, he had given over half his fortune to various philanthropic programs, among them the University of Chicago (which he principally funded) and the Rockefeller Institute for Medical Research, now Rockefeller University (founded in 1901 in New York City). The institute's program of attacking the most serious diseases of mankind gave JDR his first experience funding directly the long-term work of academically trained scientists and physicians. In 1913, Senior set up his greatest philanthropic endeavor, the Rockefeller Foundation, "to promote the well-being and to advance the civilization of the peoples of the United States. . . and of foreign lands in the acquisition and dissemination of knowledge, in the prevention and relief of human suffering, and in the promotion of any and all the elements of human progress." Today, with an endowment in excess of $2 billion, The Rockefeller Foundation remains one of the ten largest foundations in the United States.

John D. Rockefeller, Jr.
(1874–1960)

John D. Rockefeller, Jr. was born in Cleveland and moved with his family to New York City in 1884. He was the last child and only son of JDR and Laura Spelman Rockefeller. As a teenager, Junior attended day schools in the city and then, in 1893, entered Brown University in Providence, Rhode Island. There he met Abby Aldrich, who became his wife in 1901. After his 1897 graduation, Junior began to work for his father at 26 Broadway, the well-known New York City address of Standard Oil, where he learned skills in both business and philanthropy.

Building Kykuit, which he began when he was thirty-two years old, initiated Junior's lifelong involvement with building projects and historic preservation. He provided funds to restore Rheims Cathedral after it was damaged during the First World War, and Versailles, the palace of the kings of France. In 1935, closer to home, Junior bought and then donated to New York City sixty acres of land for the Cloisters in upper Manhattan, the Metropolitan Museum's medieval outpost. He paid much of the Cloister's construction cost and in 1938 donated a number of medieval sculptures and architectural fragments he had acquired from the American sculptor George Grey Barnard. (Three of Barnard's works, *The Hewer, Rising Woman,* and *Adam and Eve,* are at the base of the east terrace retaining wall at Kykuit.) The Cloisters collection includes the famed late fifteenth-century Unicorn tapestries, which once hung in Junior's New York city home on West 54th Street.

The Cloisters was not the last nor the largest of Junior's building and restoration projects. His generosity made possible some of the nation's finest historic sites and national parks. He financed the formation and development of Colonial Williamsburg beginning in the mid-1920s and then, on this model, created Sleepy Hollow Restorations, the properties that form the nucleus of Historic Hudson Valley. Philipsburg Manor and Washington Irving's home, Sunnyside, opened to the public in 1947, and Van Cortlandt Manor opened in 1959. Junior also purchased more than ten thousand acres for Acadia National Park on Maine's Mount Desert Island, where his family spent summers and where Nelson was born in 1908. His philanthropy also helped expand Wyoming's Grand Teton National Park, Virginia's Shenandoah National Park, and Tennessee's Great Smokey Mountains National Park. Junior made significant contributions to help preserve both California's redwood forests and the spectacular Palisades, the thirteen-mile stretch of cliffs between Fort Lee, New Jersey, and Nyack, New York, whose future had been threatened by intense quarrying.

Perhaps the most successful of Junior's building programs was New York City's Rockefeller Center, the most widely known project that carries the family name. The original fourteen buildings, covering three blocks between 48th and 51st Streets and between Fifth and Sixth avenues, were completed between 1930 and 1939. Rockefeller Center was the first realization of the twentieth-century ideal of a skyscraper city.

Junior was also a significant collector of art. He added throughout his life to the group of rare Chinese porcelains he had initially purchased from the J.P. Morgan estate. Some of these pieces remain at Kykuit.

Abby Greene Aldrich Rockefeller
(1874–1948)

Abby Greene Aldrich Rockefeller was the fourth of ten children of Abby Pearce Truman Chapman and Nelson Aldrich, who built his fortune in the sugar and rubber trade, banking, and public utilities. Aldrich was also an influential United States Senator from Rhode Island for thirty years.

After marrying John D. Rockefeller, Jr., Abby began to adopt and share responsibility for the family's philanthropic interests. She was also devoted to charitable concerns of her own, such as the Girl Scouts, the YWCA, and the American Red Cross, and she was crucial to the man-

Mr. and Mrs. John D. Rockefeller, Jr. at the opening of Washington Irving's Sunnyside, October 4, 1947.

agement of the family's many homes—in New York, at Tarrytown, at Seal Harbor, Maine, and at Bassett Hall, where she and her husband stayed in Colonial Williamsburg.

Abby began collecting at an early age on European trips with her father. European and Asian works were her first loves, tastes she shared with her husband. Although she and Junior also shared an enthusiasm for eighteenth-century English and French furniture and the paintings of the Old Masters, Abby Aldrich Rockefeller's other collecting ran in a very different direction. She is best known for her interest in modern art and American folk art, and her collections were unparalleled in her time or since.

She became interested in modern art after discovering the New York gallery of Edith Gregor Halpert in 1928. The next year, she was one of three women collectors who founded the Museum of Modern Art in New York City. In 1935, she donated numerous works to its collection and left the museum more works in her will. MoMA's sculpture gar-

den is named in her honor.

Perceiving substantial similarities between the modernist and folk aesthetics, Mrs. Rockefeller then began to collect folk art. She built a large and highly regarded collection of American folk art, most of which she donated to Colonial Williamsburg in 1939. The Rockefeller family financed the building in which this collection can now be seen. Mrs. Rockefeller died in New York City in 1948.

ABBY ROCKEFELLER MAUZÉ
(1903–1976)

Abby Rockefeller Mauzé was the oldest child of John D. Rockefeller, Jr. and Abby Aldrich Rockefeller. Although she chose a more private lifestyle that her brothers, she, too, was an effective philanthropist. She devoted her considerable personal resources to medical research, the search for an effective population policy, general support of the arts,

John D. Rockefeller, Jr. and Abby Aldrich Rockefeller at the opening of Philipsburg Manor, then called Philipse Castle Restoration, in 1943.

and—her great love—urban parks. She was the builder and patron of Greenacre Park, one of the first of New York's small city parks, on the Upper East Side.

JOHN D. ROCKEFELLER 3RD
(1906–1978)

The eldest son of John D. Rockefeller, Jr. and Abby Aldrich Rockefeller, John D. Rockefeller 3rd graduated from Princeton University in 1929 and spent most of his life working in philanthropy.

Taking up where his grandfather and father had left off, he continued the effort to transform philanthropy from a series of essentially idiosyncratic and often local gestures into a rational, planned, and self-conscious instrument of social change. Prior to World War II, John served as his father's representative and heir apparent on many Rockefeller boards—the Rockefeller Foundation, the Rockefeller Institute for Medical Research (now Rockefeller Univer-

sity), Colonial Williamsburg, the Davison Fund, the Spelman Fund, and more than twenty-five others, including Rockefeller Center.

After World War II, even as he retained responsibility for some of these well-established philanthropies, JDR 3rd began to direct his attention and resources to problems he considered even more critical and challenging. He became the principal force behind the effort to make American public and governmental leaders more aware of the dangers of rapid population growth; he strongly supported the efforts of Rockefeller Foundation scientists to increase the world food supply, an effort that resulted in the "Green Revolution," and to disseminate these ideas more widely; he championed the improvement of Asian-American relations, helping to revive the Japan Society and founding the Asia Society. John was a motivating force behind the creation of the Lincoln Center for the Performing Arts and was chairman of its board from 1965 to 1971. He also carried on the family's collecting tradition; with his wife, Blanchette

Hooker Rockefeller (1909-1992), he established renowned collections of American and Asian art.

NELSON ALDRICH ROCKEFELLER
(1908–1979)

Nelson Rockefeller was the third of the six children of Junior and Abby and one of the first generation of Rockefellers to be raised partly at Pocantico Hills. He and his brothers attended the Lincoln School, a division of the Teachers College of Columbia University. Nelson majored in economics at Dartmouth College, where he also studied art and landscape architecture. He graduated cum laude with a B.A. in 1930. Nelson determined at an early age not "just to work my way up in a business that another man built." He forged a unique career in international development, philanthropy, business, and public service and was especially active in the broad field of public policy. He established a distinguished record serving three presidents between 1940 and 1958 in seven different appointments. He was among other things Coordinator of Inter-American Affairs, Assistant Secretary of State under President Franklin D. Roosevelt and Under Secretary of Health, Education and Welfare, and Special Assistant to the President for Foreign Affairs under President Dwight D. Eisenhower. He was four times elected governor of New York State, serving from 1959 to 1973, and he was vice-president of the United States under Gerald Ford from 1974 to 1977.

Taught by his parents to look for and appreciate beauty in all things, Nelson shared his mother's interest in modern painting and sculpture. He began to collect art in the early 1930s and soon afterward became a trustee of both the Metropolitan Museum of Art and the Museum of Modern Art. In 1957, he founded the Museum of Primitive Art in New York City, whose collections later became part of the Metropolitan Museum.

When Nelson moved to Kykuit after his father's death in 1960, he brought part of his art collection with him and began to acquire new works to adorn the house and grounds. He commissioned a magnificent sculpture, *Large Spiny*, from Alexander Calder for one of the Kykuit terraces, and acquired others from such artists as Henry Moore, Louise Nevelson, and David Smith for different parts of the garden. At his death, he left the art collection that he had assembled in the galleries and the gardens at Kykuit to the National Trust for Historic Preservation. A major part of this collection represents the work of New York State artists of the 1960s and 1970s who had also been chosen to pro-

vide sculpture for the Albany Mall, now the Governor Nelson A. Rockefeller Empire State Plaza, the administrative and cultural complex Nelson Rockefeller developed for New York State in the 1970s. Similar in scope and intent to Rockefeller Center, the Albany Mall combines public and commercial functions in much the same way.

Nelson's passion for art was matched only by his zeal to make art accessible to the public. He promoted the inclusion of art in public spaces, and, after retiring from public life, he established The Nelson Rockefeller Collection, Inc., which produced and marketed reproductions of selected pieces from his collection.

LAURANCE SPELMAN ROCKEFELLER
(1910–2004)

Laurance Rockefeller was Junior and Abby's fourth child. Like his older brother John, he graduated from Princeton University. He was a lieutenant commander in the United States Navy during the Second World War and worked independently as a venture capitalist, philanthropist, conservationist, and resort developer.

Laurance perpetuated the Rockefeller family's long interest in medical research. He led the effort in 1960 to create the Memorial Sloan-Kettering Cancer Center and served as the Center's chairman from 1960 to 1982. He also continued the family's involvement in the preservation of scenic lands and was instrumental in the creation of the Virgin Islands National Park on St. John, and with his wife Mary French Rockefeller, he helped create the first National Park in Vermont, the Marsh-Billings National Historical Park in Woodstock. Laurance's interest in scenic lands long embraced a deep commitment to conservation; as early as 1940, he was head of Jackson Hole Preserve, Inc., a conservation organization that helps protect the Grand Tetons and California's redwood trees. In 1958, he founded the American Conservation Association, and he served under five presidents as an advisor on conservation and outdoor recreation.

A pioneer in venture capital investment, Laurance concentrated on new enterprises operating on technological frontiers. His investment interests included aeronautics, optics, high temperature physics, composite materials, lasers, computers, and data processing. Companies that owe their early success to his investments include Eastern Airlines, Intel, McDonnell Aircraft Company, and Apple Computer. As founder of Rockresorts, Inc., Laurance built a successful chain of international resort hotels, each one integrated into its surroundings in an environmentally sensitive

The children of Mr. and Mrs. John D. Rockefeller, Jr.: Abby (Babs), John D. 3rd, Nelson, Laurance, Winthrop, and David, about 1917.

manner. His work in medical research, conservation, and environmental protection was cited in 1990 when President George Bush awarded him the Congressional Gold Medal; a year later Princeton gave Rockefeller its highest alumni recognition, the Woodrow Wilson Award, for his service to the university and the nation. In 1990, he established the Center for Human Values at Princeton, whose mission fosters ongoing inquiry into important ethical issues in private and public life.

WINTHROP ROCKEFELLER
(1912–1973)

Winthrop Rockefeller, Junior and Abby's fifth child, attended Yale University and worked in the oil refinery industry from the mid-1930s until the early 1950s (except during the war years, when he advanced from private to lieutenant colonel in the United States Army). After becoming a successful rancher in Arkansas in the 1950s, he turned his attention to industrial development and public policy issues in that state. He served on the Republican National Committee from Arkansas (from 1961) and was elected to two terms as governor of Arkansas (1967 to 1971), becoming its first Republican governor since Reconstruction. Winthrop also was a director of the Rockefeller

Brothers Fund and Rockefeller Center and chairman of Colonial Williamsburg from 1953 until his death in 1973.

DAVID ROCKEFELLER
(1915–)

David Rockefeller is the sixth child and youngest son of John D. Rockefeller, Jr. and Abby Aldrich Rockefeller. Born in 1915, he graduated from Harvard College in 1936, and then studied at the London School of Economics and took his Ph.D. in economics in 1940 from the University of Chicago. He served as an intelligence officer during World War II in North Africa and France and as an assistant military attaché in Paris soon after its liberation.

After the war, Rockefeller joined the Chase National Bank, a position from which he effectively advocated a stronger international presence for American banks and greater participation on the part of the United States in the process of economic development around the world—causes to which his brother Nelson was also dedicated. He rose through the ranks at the new Chase Manhattan Bank, becoming president in 1960 and chairman and chief executive officer in 1969. David was principally responsible for the bank's decision to remain on Wall Street and to symbolize that decision with a radical new headquarters designed in the

Genealogical Chart of the Rockefeller Family

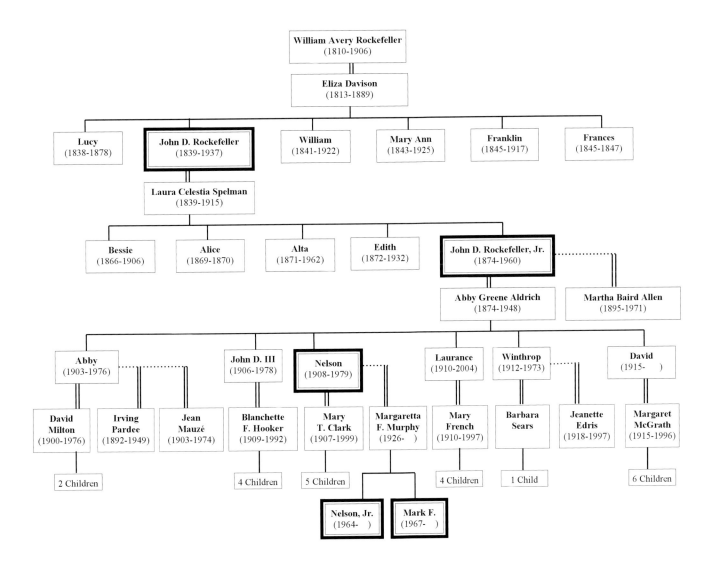

international style. During David's tenure, the bank became a global financial institution reflecting the changing nature of the world economy and his own vision. David has been a significant statesman; he founded the Trilateral Commission and participated in many international organizations, including the Council on Foreign Relations, which he chaired for fifteen years. Closer to home, he helped establish the New York City Partnership and has served on other boards concerned with improving the quality of life in the city.

With his siblings, David has continued the Rockefeller family's strong tradition of philanthropy. He has been on the Rockefeller University board for more than fifty years and was its chair for twenty-five years. Like his mother and brother Nelson, he chaired the board of the

Museum of Modern Art on two separate occasions. He and his wife Peggy also assembled one of the nation's great collections of modern art.

In 2004, David Rockefeller established the Stone Barns Center for Food and Agriculture, in Pocantico Hills, New York, in honor of his wife Peggy, who died in 1996. The Center's mission is to demonstrate, teach, and promote sustainable, community-based food production, a long-time interest of Peggy Rockefeller, who was a founder of the American Farmland Trust.

PHOTOGRAPH AND PICTURE CREDITS

ACKNOWLEDGMENTS

This guidebook is based largely on the text written by Henry Joyce for the first edition of the guidebook to Kykuit, published in 1994. Mr. Joyce relied on the work of Hugh J. McCauley, architect and historian, who prepared Kykuit's historic structures report, and the work of Albert Berger, who wrote the first in-depth work on the history of the site in 1982 for Historic Hudson Valley. Appreciation was expressed to Cynthia Bronson Altman, curator at Kykuit, and the staff of Pocantico Programs of the Rockefeller Brothers Fund: Charles Granquist, director of Pocantico Programs, Judy Clark, associate director, and Kimberly Miller, assistant director of operations.

The Rockefeller Archive Center, especially Dr. Darwin Stapleton, director, and Melissa A. Smith, archivist, were particularly helpful to Mr. Joyce. Furthermore, we extended our gratitude to HHV's trustees at the time, including then chairman Richard Gilder, Clayton W. Frye, Jr., and Frances D. Fergusson and her committee. The National Trust and Historic Hudson Valley were especially grateful to members of the Rockefeller family and many of their associates for information and guidance in the preparation of the first edition of the guidebook.

For this second edition of the Kykuit guidebook, our thanks go to Mark F. Rockefeller, chairman of Historic Hudson Valley, for a foreword that highlights Kykuit's relevance to both the Rockefeller family and visitors from around the world. Great appreciation goes to Cynthia Bronson Altman, curator at Kykuit, for additional, original text and extensive help and support. Sincere appreciation is extended to George Ellsworth Shear for his generosity in allowing us to use his beautiful architectural images of Hudson Valley historic sites on the inside front and inside back covers of this publication.

Much gratitude goes to my colleagues at Historic Hudson Valley: Kathleen Eagen Johnson, curator, and Margaret L. Vetare, director of interpretation, for their sage advice; Karen M. Sharman, director of human resources, for new color photography, additional editing, and ongoing encouragement; Ruth Merrill, operations manager for the Kykuit program, for fact checking and additional photo caption text; and Henri Corbacho, director of retail operations, for his foresight and encouragement. Appreciation is extended to Louise O'Rourke, administrative assistant at Historic Hudson Valley, for computer assistance; and to Aimée Ducey, curatorial assistant at Kykuit, for her timely help. Thanks also go to others at Historic Hudson Valley who provided sensitive support and counsel: David M. Parsons, director of finance and administration, and McKelden Smith, director of marketing; and to Waddell W. Stillman, president, whose patience and intelligent guidance in pursuit of this second edition was instrumental in the completion of the project.

Once again we are grateful to the Rockefeller Archive Center, especially Dr. Darwin Stapleton, director, as well as Ken Rose, assistant director, and Amy Fitch, Mindy Gordon, and Michele Hiltzik, archivists, for their additional research and gracious response to our queries.

SUSAN T. GREENSTEIN
Director, Kykuit Program
Historic Hudson Valley

WELCOME TO THE EXTRAORDINARY LANDMARKS OF
SLEEPY HOLLOW COUNTRY AND THE GREAT ESTATES REGION

Visitors to Sleepy Hollow Country discover one of the most important and richly varied concentrations of historic landmarks in the country. Of these sites, the principal landmarks are largely properties of Historic Hudson Valley and The National Trust for Historic Preservation. Each of these sites feature guided tours that bring to life the stories and legacy of past generations.

Historic Hudson Valley is an acknowledged leader in the field of historic preservation and education. In 1951, John D. Rockefeller, Jr. founded Historic Hudson Valley as a non-profit educational organization called Sleepy Hollow Restorations. The organization's mission is to preserve the culture, landscape, and history of the Hudson River Valley, and to present this heritage to the public through daily tours, school programs, special events, publications, a website, and other programs. For more information about visiting the historic sites of Sleepy Hollow Country and the Great Estates Region, please visit Historic Hudson Valley online at www.hudsonvalley.org or telephone us at 914-631-8200.

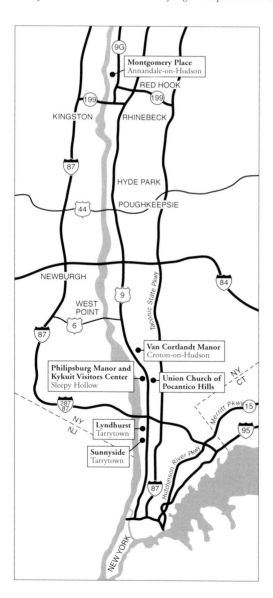

WASHINGTON IRVING'S SUNNYSIDE

If one estate truly captures the gracious and picturesque aspects of the Hudson River Valley, it is Washington Irving's Sunnyside. The author of *The Legend of Sleepy Hollow and Rip Van Winkle* designed this romantic riverfront home beginning in 1835. Woodland walks, colorful gardens planted with many heirloom species, scenic picnic areas, delightful views of the Hudson River, and an appealing Museum Shop enhance a visit to this must-see National Historic Landmark. A property of Historic Hudson Valley.

PHILIPSBURG MANOR

Philipsburg Manor is a colonial-era milling and trading complex that was owned by a Dutch family of merchants and operated by a community of enslaved individuals of African descent. A working, water-powered gristmill, live demonstrations of traditional colonial activities, and historic breeds of farm animals help reveal the story of those who lived and labored at Philipsburg Manor circa 1750. The Visitor Center, with its Greenhouse Café and Museum Shop, serves as the starting point for all tours to Kykuit. A property of Historic Hudson Valley.

KYKUIT, THE ROCKEFELLER ESTATE

Overlooking the broad expanse of the Tappan Zee, Kykuit was the home to four generations of the Rockefeller family. The six-story stone house commands stunning views of the Hudson River and the Palisades. The surrounding Beaux-Arts gardens, set amidst a sweeping romantic landscape, feature extensive terraces, fountains, and twentieth-century sculpture collected by Governor Nelson A. Rockefeller. Kykuit is a historic site of the National Trust and is maintained and administered by the Rockefeller Brothers Fund as a center for its philanthropic programs. Historic Hudson Valley operates public programs at Kykuit. The Visitor Center at Philipsburg Manor serves as the starting point for all Kykuit tours.

THE UNION CHURCH OF POCANTICO HILLS

Set in the context of a stone church on a quiet country road, a rose window by Henri Matisse and nine stained glass windows by Marc Chagall, commissioned by members of the Rockefeller family, create dramatic combinations of light and color and provide unique views of these two twentieth-century art masters. The rose window was Matisse's last work; the Chagall windows are his only cycle of church windows in America. A property of Historic Hudson Valley.

VAN CORTLANDT MANOR

Nestled between the gentle Croton River and a forested ridge, Van Cortlandt Manor exemplifies a vivid picture of the domestic country life of a patriot family in the newly independent United States, circa 1800. The stone manor house features one of the few collections of eighteenth-century furniture and household objects surviving in their original setting. The brick, ferry house tavern reveals a wide variety of regional vernacular furnishings. Live demonstrations of period crafts and tasks occur daily. Beautiful gardens, a riverside picnic area, and charming Museum Shop invite visitors to linger. A property of Historic Hudson Valley.

LYNDHURST

One of America's great domestic landmarks, Lyndhurst is a Gothic Revival-style mansion designed in two stages by architect A.J. Davis, who also created many of the furnishings. The grounds include a picturesque, park-like landscape with magnificent specimen trees, splendid views of the Tappan Zee, gardens, the remains of an immense, nineteenth-century greenhouse, and the restored carriage house. A historic site of the National Trust.

MONTGOMERY PLACE HISTORIC ESTATE

This breathtaking nineteenth-century estate includes hundreds of unspoiled acres overlooking the Hudson River and Catskill Mountains, expansive and varied gardens and grounds, nature trails, the dramatic waterfalls of the Sawkill, a Museum Shop, and fresh fruit for sale in season at the Montgomery Place Orchards farm stand. The eminent nineteenth-century architect, A.J. Davis, designed the neo-classical style house and several outbuildings. A property of Historic Hudson Valley.